# LAND ROVER

## SERIES I, II, IIA & III

# LAND ROVER
## SERIES I, II, IIA & III

BY JAMES TAYLOR

Herridge & Sons

Published in 2013 by
Herridge & Sons Ltd
Lower Forda, Shebbear
Devon EX21 5SY

Reprinted 2021

Design by Ray Leaning, MUSE Fine Art & Design

ISBN 978-1-906133-51-1
Printed in China

# CONTENTS

# INTRODUCTION

In the six and a half decades since its introduction in April 1948, the Land Rover has become a legend. Today, Land Rover relies on that legend to sell its current models, which have built on the achievements of the original vehicle but now have a very different kind of appeal. In the beginning, the Land Rover was a light commercial vehicle, not a lifestyle statement, and its makers used all the familiar tools of advertising and illustrated catalogues to promote its merits to would-be buyers.

Those catalogues themselves have attracted a following of collectors, and there is no doubt that they have a very special fascination. Over the years, styles and customer expectations have changed, and the catalogues reflect those changes as much as they reflect changes in the specification and appearance of the vehicles themselves. They appeal on several levels – as attractive period-pieces, as a historical record, and in many cases as a visual feast.

There have of course been hundreds of different sales catalogues since 1948, in many different languages. Some of them are now exceptionally rare and correspondingly expensive – although they were of course given away free through Land Rover dealers when new. All those illustrated in this book come from my own collection, which has been put together over a period of around 35 years with a lot of assistance from well-wishers and fellow enthusiasts.

Between 1948 and 1983, the Land Rover changed at an incredibly slow rate. It gained more powerful engines, alternative engines, alternative sizes and a simply massive array of bolt-on accessories and conversion options – but the basic vehicle always remained true to the original concept. From 1983, the original was progressively replaced by a more modern design that featured coil-spring suspension instead of leaf springs, and permanent four-wheel drive instead of the selectable type that had characterised most of the marque's early years. By the end of 1985, the original had gone, and this book focuses on that original, leaving the coil-sprung models for another time and another volume.

Though Land Rover today is recognised as a company in its own right (most recently half of Jaguar Land Rover, now owned by the Indian Tata group), it was originally simply a product of the old Rover Company. Rover, which was absorbed into British Leyland in the 1960s, was a small but respected maker of up-market motor cars. By the end of the Second World War, it was keen to tackle the challenge of the immediate post-war years but was not prepared for the British Government's focus on export. Rover had never taken markets outside the UK very seriously at all, and it had to set up an export organisation very quickly. With no new designs yet ready, it tried to sell revitalised pre-war designs both at home and abroad, but the world had moved on. Outside the countries of the British Commonwealth, where the market was closer to being a captive one, it made very little headway.

This looked like becoming a real problem, because the Government was threatening to allocate supplies of steel (then in short supply) to manufacturers on the basis of their export performance. Rover needed an export product quickly if it was not going to be starved of raw materials, and its Chief Engineer, Maurice Wilks, hit upon the idea of building a vehicle similar to the wartime US Jeep, but intended for agricultural and light industrial work. He knew how useful such a spartan runabout could be, as he had bought a war-surplus example himself and experimented with it in the grounds of his Midlands home and in the countryside and on the beaches of Anglesey, where he owned a holiday cottage.

This idea received the approval of the Rover Board in 1947, and by early 1948 the first prototypes of the new vehicle were up and running. It had picked up the name Land Rover, which both linked it to the Rover Company and made clear what its intended use was. First displayed at the Amsterdam Motor Show in 1948, that choice reflecting to a large extent the intention of attracting overseas orders, the new Land Rover was a huge success. Demand took the Rover Company by surprise, and the vehicle that they had hastily put together to tide them through a bad period ended up becoming their most important product line. By 1951, it was out-selling Rover cars by two to one and, although the Rover Board never admitted it in so many words, from that time on it was the Land Rover that became the company's primary product, with the cars as something of a sideline.

One reason why the Land Rover developed so slowly was that Rover had to put most of its resources into gearing up production to meet demand. Changes to the specification were developed piecemeal, and such things as engines tended to change only when Land Rovers and cars shared a common need, so that development and manufacturing costs could be shared as much as possible. Partly because of pressure on manufacturing resources, but also to get around prohibitive import tariffs, Land Rovers were also shipped overseas in kit form from early on. This of course also inhibited specification changes to a degree, because there was always a time delay between the arrival of a new design and the ability to get it assembled into complete vehicles abroad.

| Year | Petrol | | Diesel | SWB | | LWB | | Forward control LWB only | |
|---|---|---|---|---|---|---|---|---|---|
| 1948 | 1.6 4cyl | | | 80" | | | | | Series I introduced |
| 1949 | 1.6 4cyl | | | 80" | | | | | |
| 1950 | 1.6 4cyl | | | 80" | | | | | |
| 1951 | 1.6 4cyl | 2.0 4cyl | | 80" | | | | | |
| 1952 | | 2.0 4cyl | | 80" | | | | | |
| 1953 | | 2.0 4cyl | | 80" | 86" | 107" | | | |
| 1954 | | 2.0 4cyl * | | | 86" | 107" | | | |
| 1955 | | 2.0 4cyl * | | | 86" | 107" | | | |
| 1956 | | 2.0 4cyl * | | | 86" | 88" | 107" | 109" | |
| 1957 | | 2.0 4cyl * | 2.0 4cyl | | | 88" | | 109" | |
| 1958 | | 2.0 4cyl * | 2.0 4cyl | | | 88" | | 109" | |
| | *modified bore spacing | | | | | | | | |
| 1958 | 2.25 4cyl* | | 2.0 4cyl | 88" | | 109" | | | Series II introduced |
| 1959 | 2.25 4cyl | | 2.0 4cyl | 88" | | 109" | | | |
| 1960 | 2.25 4cyl | | 2.0 4cyl | 88" | | 109" | | | |
| 1961 | 2.25 4cyl | | 2.0 4cyl | 88" | | 109" | | | |
| 1961 | 2.25 4cyl | | 2.25 4cyl | 88" | | 109" | | | Series IIA introduced |
| 1962 | 2.25 4cyl | | 2.25 4cyl | 88" | | 109" | | | |
| 1963 | 2.25 4cyl | 2.6 6cyl ** | 2.25 4cyl | 88" | | 109" | | 109" | |
| 1964 | 2.25 4cyl | 2.6 6cyl ** | 2.25 4cyl | 88" | | 109" | | 109" | |
| 1965 | 2.25 4cyl | 2.6 6cyl ** | 2.25 4cyl | 88" | | 109" | | 109" | |
| 1966 | 2.25 4cyl | 2.6 6cyl ** | 2.25 4cyl | 88" | | 109" | | 110" | |
| 1967 | 2.25 4cyl | 2.6 6cyl | 2.25 4cyl | 88" | | 109" | | 110" | |
| 1968 | 2.25 4cyl | 2.6 6cyl | 2.25 4cyl | 88" | | 109" | | 110" | |
| 1969 | 2.25 4cyl | 2.6 6cyl | 2.25 4cyl | 88" | | 109" | | 110" | |
| 1970 | 2.25 4cyl | 2.6 6cyl | 2.25 4cyl | 88" | | 109" | | 110" | |
| 1971 | 2.25 4cyl | 2.6 6cyl | 2.25 4cyl | 88" | | 109" | | 110" | |
| | *The very first Series II 88s had the 2.0 litre 4cyl engine | | | **Export only | | | | | |
| 1971 | 2.25 4cyl | 2.6 6cyl | 2.25 4cyl | 88" | | 109" | | | Series III introduced |
| 1972 | 2.25 4cyl | 2.6 6cyl | 2.25 4cyl | 88" | | 109" | | | |
| 1973 | 2.25 4cyl | 2.6 6cyl | 2.25 4cyl | 88" | | 109" | | | |
| 1974 | 2.25 4cyl | 2.6 6cyl | 2.25 4cyl | 88" | | 109" | | | |
| 1975 | 2.25 4cyl | 2.6 6cyl | 2.25 4cyl | 88" | | 109" | | | |
| 1976 | 2.25 4cyl | 2.6 6cyl | 2.25 4cyl | 88" | | 109" | | | |
| 1977 | 2.25 4cyl | 2.6 6cyl | 2.25 4cyl | 88" | | 109" | | | |
| 1978 | 2.25 4cyl | 3.5 V8 | 2.25 4cyl | 88" | | 109" | | | |
| 1979 | 2.25 4cyl | 3.5 V8 | 2.25 4cyl | 88" | | 109" | | | |
| 1980 | 2.25 4cyl | 3.5 V8 | 2.25 4cyl | 88" | | 109" | | | |
| 1981 | 2.25 4cyl | 3.5 V8 | 2.25 4cyl | 88" | | 109" | | | |
| 1982 | 2.25 4cyl | 3.5 V8 | 2.25 4cyl | 88" | | 109" | | | |
| 1983* | 2.25 4cyl | 3.5 V8 | 2.25 4cyl | 88" | | 109" | | | |
| | *Deliveries of orders previously placed for leaf spring models by the military and other organisations continue until 1985 | | | | | | | | |

# FIRST THOUGHTS

Once Maurice Wilks had settled on the idea of creating a light four-wheel-drive runabout that would bring in those much-needed export sales for Rover, he

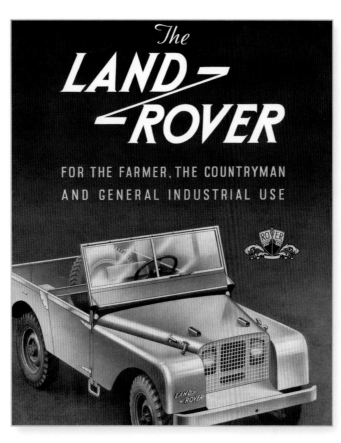

*This was the cover of the very first Land Rover sales brochure, issued at the Amsterdam Show in April 1948. The picture has been heavily airbrushed – "re-arted" was the term in use at Solihull – from an original photograph of the experimental "Centre-Steer" model. Most of it looks like the production vehicles, but the steering wheel is still unmistakeably in the middle. Details such as the curved valance behind the bumper were not carried over to production, and the "step" just ahead of the door is pure fiction.*

*This is the original photograph on which that first sales brochure's cover was based. It was taken outside the admin block at Rover's Solihull factory, probably in mid-January 1948. The photographer was John Toft-Bate, a commercial photographer from Leamington Spa who had a contract with Rover at the time.*

decided to try his ideas out in the metal. As far as we know, the first stage was to put a Rover engine into a Jeep, and that was known as Project J. The engine was probably a prototype of the new post-war Rover IOE (Inlet Over Exhaust) type and most likely a 12hp derivative. The Jeep would have been an Army surplus vehicle, and may well have been the very one that Wilks had bought from his neighbour early in 1947.

That seemed to work, and so the next stage was to create a more advanced version, this time with a body built by Rover and other improvements. This second experimental model was built in the Jig Shop at Solihull over the summer of 1947, and it was completed by the end of September. It may have been constructed from the Project J vehicle; we don't know for sure, but it was certainly built on a Jeep chassis. We do know that Wilks used it to try out an idea that sounded very good in theory. To save the cost and complication of building vehicles with both right-hand and left-hand drive for different export markets, he decided to try putting the steering wheel in the middle to suit all markets.

In the mean time, Wilks had instructed the Drawing Office to do the "proper" design for what had already been christened the Land Rover. He established a development team led by Arthur Goddard, and obviously handed over the "Centre-Steer" vehicle to them. They were unimpressed by the central steering wheel idea; Goddard, who was a tall man, remembered that it left no space for the driver's legs, while junior engineer Tom Barton remembered that hand signals (which were required by law in those days) were invisible to following drivers when the hood was erected.

So the "Centre-Steer" vehicle barely figured in the development programme, and as soon as the first pre-production Land Rovers became available in March 1948, it was probably sidelined altogether. Nevertheless, Rover had committed to showing the new Land Rover at the Amsterdam Show at the end of April, and they needed sales brochures to give out. Lead-times meant that work on the brochure had to begin before there were any "real" Land Rovers to photograph.

It was Rover practice in the early post-war years – and for many years afterwards, too – to employ commercial artists to design and illustrate their sales brochures. In this case, those commercial artists were given photographs of the experimental "Centre-Steer" vehicle, were probably shown drawings of the planned production Land Rover, and were left to do their best. As a result, the first Land Rover sales brochure had no pictures at all of real Land Rovers. Instead, it had a series of airbrushed pictures that had started life as photographs of Maurice Wilks' "Centre-Steer".

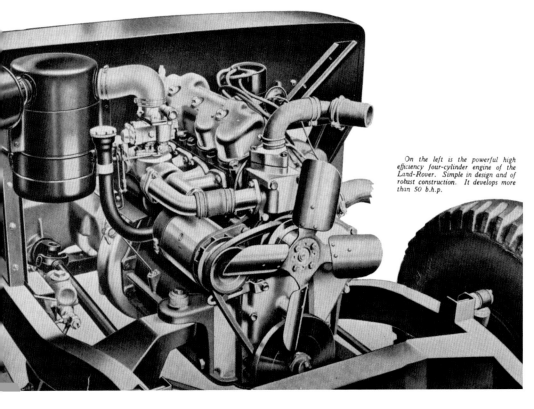

On the left is the powerful high efficiency four-cylinder engine of the Land-Rover. Simple in design and of robust construction. It develops more than 50 b.h.p.

This at least is authentic! Based either on a photograph or on a cutaway demonstration engine, this shows the combustion chamber arrangement of the new post-war Rover engine. The inlet valve is over-head, the exhaust valve at the side, and the spark plug is right in the middle of the combustion chamber. The piston top is domed and in reality was less pointed than it appears here. The IOE (Inlet Over Exhaust) engine was usually known as the Sloping Head type at Rover, for reasons which are obvious from this illustration.

This picture certainly shows a Rover IOE (Inlet Over Exhaust) engine as used in production models, although whether it is the production 1.6-litre type or not is impossible to tell. However, that bulkhead behind it is certainly not a production type, and the production chassis side members were very noticeably more substantial than these. Almost certainly, this is another "re-arted" photograph of the experimental "Centre-Steer". Sadly, the original is missing.

Whatever else this was, it was most certainly not a production-type Land Rover chassis! The layout was essentially the same, and that does look like a Rover engine and gearbox. Most experts think this was the Jeep chassis fitted with Rover running-gear, but unfortunately the original photograph on which it was based has not been found. There had been a certain amount of "re-arting", of course: the Jeep's chassis had channel-section side-members, and these are box-section members as would be used on production Land Rovers.

De buitengewoon sterke uitvoering van het Landrover chassis wordt op nevenstaande afbeelding treffend aangetoond. De zeer zware uitvoering en de robuuste motor komen hier duidelijk tot hun recht.

De aandrijving van de rear power take-off geschiedt door de hoofd versnellingsbak, terwijl de voor- en achterwiel aandrijving vanuit de transfer-box plaats vindt.

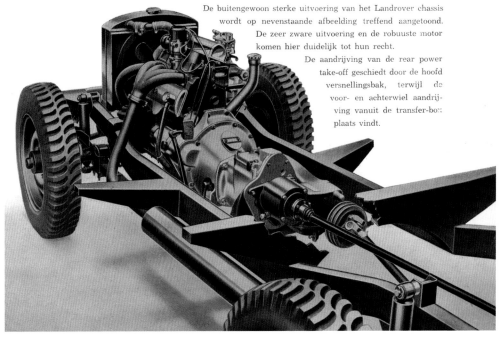

This is probably that same chassis again; the "re-arting" is obvious in the cutaway cross-member that makes the rear of the transmission visible. The pedal to the left of the bell-housing has a production Rover car-type rubber with ornate R moulded into its surface, but its position is suspect. It is not the accelerator pedal of a LHD model, but a clutch pedal – and that identifies this as the Centre-Steer chassis. Once again, no original photograph has yet been found to help confirm this.

*Maurice Wilks envisaged the Land Rover driving farm machinery from its power take-offs, and this illustration shows an example driving a hay conveyor by belt from a pulley on its rear power take-off. However, the artist's airbrush has been at work again here …*

De roestvrije licht metalen carrosserie tezamen met de gegalvaniseerde stalen verbindingsstukken van het exterieur, verzekeren lage onderhoudskosten.

Hier ziet U de Land-rover met rear power take-off als aandrijver voor een Jacobslad-der.

*… and this is the original photograph, which actually shows the experimental "Centre-Steer". It was probably taken at Foredrove Farm behind the Rover factory in mid-October 1947. At this stage, the Centre-Steer was still being used to prove the soundness of Maurice Wilks' original concept.*

Hier ziet U de Landrover als een snel en economisch voertuig. De Landrover kan naar verkiezing met links of rechts stuur geleverd worden.

*Both of these illustrations were based on original photographs of the Centre-Steer, and those original photographs still survive to prove it. The older man driving the vehicle is thought to have been the farmer at Foredrove Farm; the younger man has been identified as his son. The trailer was a war-surplus American military type (a Willys MBT or Bantam BT3) that would typically have been towed behind a Jeep during the recent war.*

DEZE AFBEELDINGEN VERTELLEN HUN EIGEN GESCHIE-DENIS

*The Land Rover demonstrates its ability to power farm machinery again here, driving a saw-bench from its rear power take-off. This is another "re-arted" picture, and the details of the rear cross-member and tailboard are not at all convincing. The trailer is the same war-surplus type seen with milk churns in another picture.*

*Cross-country ability was a key feature of the new Land Rover, and this picture was intended to illustrate that. It is based on a photograph of the "Centre-Steer" that was taken at the end of January 1948.*

ACTION!

*Action indeed: the scene is the ford at Packington Park, near Solihull, and the position of the driver makes clear that the original picture must have shown the "Centre-Steer". Once again, the artist has been at work with his airbrush.*

11

# EARLY PRODUCTION: 1948

Rover's aim was to get the Land Rover into full production as quickly as possible, to get overseas sales moving and earn both the revenue that came from that and the approval from the Ministry of Supply that would guarantee further supplies of rationed raw materials. The original plan was to build 50 pre-production models for testing – a far greater number than the company normally made for a new car, but this was of course a totally new and untried model. In practice, just 48 pre-production Land Rovers were built because no more were needed: development and testing had demonstrated that the concept was right and so volume production began in June 1948.

All new vehicles need a handbook, and this was the one prepared for the new Land Rover. The drawing clearly shows the real thing, but its angle also suggests that its origins might lie in that January 1948 picture of the experimental "Centre-Steer" that was "re-arted" for the first sales brochure. Interesting is that the vehicle is pictured with left-hand drive: Rover were clearly taking the export business very seriously indeed! This handbook was once the property of Gordon Bashford, the design engineer responsible for the original chassis. The sticker reading "R.31" at top left was the reference number for the technical library he kept in his office at Solihull.

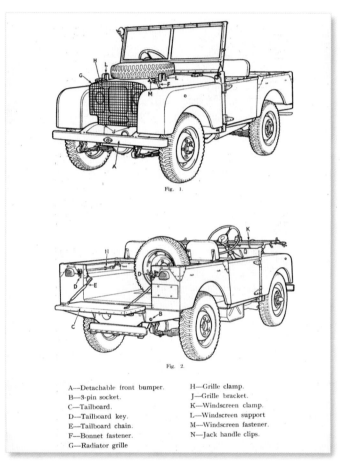

A—Detachable front bumper.
B—3-pin socket.
C—Tailboard.
D—Tailboard key.
E—Tailboard chain.
F—Bonnet fastener.
G—Radiator grille.
H—Grille clamp.
J—Grille bracket.
K—Windscreen clamp.
L—Windscreen support.
M—Windscreen fastener.
N—Jack handle clips.

Even so, the drawings inside the handbook showed a right-hand-drive model. This was the real thing: the book was printed in June 1948 and the artist would have had time to study a pre-production model thoroughly to produce his drawings. This really is a pre-production model, too. Just visible below the door in the upper picture is the long silencer of the P3 car exhaust system used on early pre-production models. This was changed for a transverse rear silencer before production began. The seats are the pre-production type which were really just backrests bolted to the top of the transom panel – although they seem more substantial in this drawing than they were in reality. Only one spare wheel was supplied, but the artist has shown it in its standard position behind the seats and in the optional position on the bonnet as well.

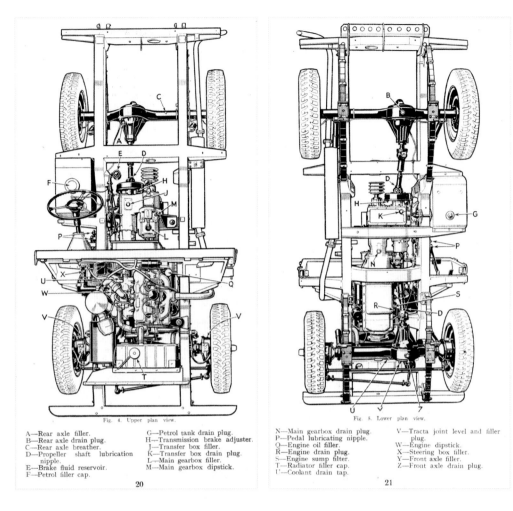

Fig. 4. Upper plan view.    Fig. 5. Lower plan view.

20

A—Rear axle filler.
B—Rear axle drain plug.
C—Rear axle breather.
D—Propeller shaft lubrication nipple.
E—Brake fluid reservoir.
F—Petrol filler cap.
G—Petrol tank drain plug.
H—Transmission brake adjuster.
J—Transfer box filler.
K—Transfer box drain plug.
L—Main gearbox filler.
M—Main gearbox dipstick.

21

N—Main gearbox drain plug.
P—Pedal lubricating nipple.
Q—Engine oil filler.
R—Engine drain plug.
S—Engine sump filter.
T—Radiator filler cap.
U—Coolant drain tap.
V—Tracta joint level and filler plug.
W—Engine dipstick.
X—Steering box filler.
Y—Front axle filler.
Z—Front axle drain plug.

*The chassis layout drawings from that very first handbook show all the essential features of the first Land Rovers. The P3 car silencer is in evidence here, and runs uncomfortably close to the rear wheel. This probably explains why it was changed. Later printings of the handbook, from October 1948, showed the new transverse silencer.*

## CONTROLS AND INSTRUMENTS

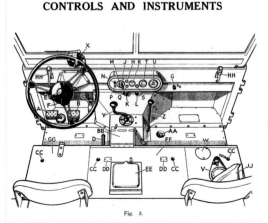

Fig. 3.

A—Clutch pedal.
B—Brake pedal.
C—Accelerator pedal.
D—Hand-brake.
E—Horn button.
F—Headlamp dipper switch.
G—Mixture control.
H—Mixture control warning light.
J—Ignition switch.
K—Starter switch.
L—Slow-running control.
M—Lamp switch.
N—Instrument panel light switch
P—Lead lamp socket.
Q—Charging warning light.
R—Ammeter.
S—Oil pressure warning light.
T—Petrol level gauge.

U—Speedometer.
V—Petrol filler cap.
W—Access plate for petrol level unit.
X—Windscreen wiper.
Y—Main gear-change lever.
Z—Transfer box change lever.
AA—Freewheel control.
BB—Access cover for gear-box filler.
CC—Location hole for seat.
DD—Cover plate for seat location hole.
EE—Access cover for power take-off control.
FF—Hinged seat-box lid.
GG—Tool-box.
HH—Windscreen clamp.
JJ—Access cover for petrol filler.

*In the very beginning, the Land Rover was offered for sale with almost everything as an extra-cost option – including the doors and a spare wheel. It soon became apparent that customers didn't like that idea very much, and so the doors and spare wheel were standardised, and the price went up from £450 to £540, the difference being a lot more than the cost of the newly standardised parts.*

*The very early seats are in evidence again on this drawing of the controls. Instruments in the centre reduced differences between RHD and LHD models, although Rover cars had featured central instruments for some years. The main gear lever was cranked left or right, to suit, and the handbrake simply moved to the other side of the transmission tunnel. The transfer box lever was always in the same place, and so was the ring-pull for the freewheel control. The freewheel was a long-standing Rover car device that had been adapted to suit the Land Rover; it was used to disconnect drive to the front axle, so avoiding transmission "wind-up". When drive was needed to all four wheels, the freewheel was set to its fixed-drive position.*

# ADDED VALUE, 1948-1953

Right from the start, the Land Rover had been conceived as a basic platform to which users added the items they wanted. Power take-offs were in the plan from the beginning, as Rover expected their new vehicle to be used to drive farm machinery just like a steam traction engine. In the light industrial field, however, the situation was different. Items of machinery needed to be mounted to the vehicle itself and driven from its power take-offs.

The Land Rover on Rover's stand at the Amsterdam Motor Show in April 1948 anticipated such industrial requirements, and was equipped as a mobile welder. Once production began, it became clear that the welder required special attention on the assembly lines, and so Rover gave the model its own chassis number series. It was followed by a mobile compressor variant, though this was numbered in the standard series.

Quite early on, it became clear that users needed more load space in their Land Rovers, and so Rover arranged with specialist manufacturer Brockhouse of West Bromwich to design and build a trailer that used Land Rover wheels and had the same track as a Land Rover so that it could follow it easily across muddy or rutted ground. It was also Brockhouse, incidentally, who had built the special car transporter trailers that Rover used for a time in the early 1950s to move new vehicles around the country, although in later years the job was sub-contracted to vehicle movement specialists.

*For driving machinery mounted on the vehicle itself, the usual choice was a Centre Power Take-Off or CPTO. This cost extra. It was driven directly from the gearbox; the main gearbox was put into neutral and the lever shown in these illustrations transferred drive to the PTO. The drive was transferred to the machinery by three rubber belts running on pulleys.*

The Welder required quite a lot of extra work on the assembly lines, including provision of an oil cooler. By 1953, Rover had decided that such vehicles needed to be completed away from the main assembly lines, where fitting the special equipment was simply too disruptive. Looking for a suitably dramatic picture to illustrate a welder in action, and presumably not finding one, Rover asked their commercial artist to produce one. The registration number GWD 252 belonged to a 1948 Rover P3 model. Was that perhaps the number of the artist's own vehicle?

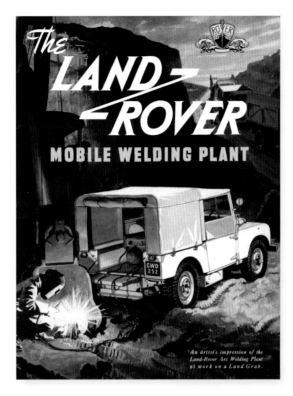

An artist's impression of the Land-Rover Arc Welding Plant at work on a Land Grab.

Land-Rover arc welding plant at work in the factory.

Land-Rover mobile arc welding plant fully equipped.

THE rear power take-off of the Land-Rover is of robust construction designed for many jobs on the Farm and in Industry and enables power to be taken just where it is wanted. It is driven through the main shaft of the main gear box. The pulley unit as shown provides belt drive for circular saws, elevators, and other belt driven machinery. This unit is easily detachable exposing a splined shaft (see overleaf) for operating implements requiring positive drive.

| | |
|---|---|
| Land-Rover with standard equipment as list | £540 |
| REAR POWER TAKE-OFF | £20 |
| PULLEY UNIT | £15 |
| ENGINE GOVERNOR (ESSENTIAL) | £15 |

**£590** COMPLETE  Delivery ex-Works
Subject to alteration without notice NOV/49.

E & O.E.

IN this illustration the Rear Power Take-off Pulley Unit is removed showing the splined positive drive shaft for driving machinery requiring positive non-slip drive; a cowl is fitted to provide protection.

PRICE

| | |
|---|---|
| Land-Rover with standard equipment as list | £540 |
| REAR POWER TAKE-OFF WITHOUT PULLEY UNIT | £20 |

**£560** COMPLETE Delivery ex-Works
Subject to alteration without notice NOV/49.

E. & O. E.

**THE ROVER COMPANY LIMITED**
SOLIHULL • BIRMINGHAM • ENGLAND
Telephone: Sheldon 2451.    Telegrams: Rover, Solihull.
Service Depot: SOLIHULL.  Telegrams: Rovrepair, Solihull.  London Showrooms: DEVONSHIRE HOUSE, PICCADILLY, W.1.  Telephone: Grosvenor 3252.  London Service Depot: SEAGRAVE ROAD, FULHAM, S.W.6.  Telephone: Fulham 1231.  Telegrams: Rovrepair  Phone Fulham
The name Land-Rover is a registered Trade mark of the Rover Company Limited

It's easy to see from these pictures why finding a suitably dramatic picture of the welder in action was a problem; there is absolutely no drama about the pictures here, which may well have been taken by John Toft-Bate, the industrial photographer from Leamington Spa who did all of Rover's early post-war work until the company established its own photographic department.

For driving free-standing machinery, a rear power take-off (RPTO) was available at extra cost. Like the CPTO, this was an extra-cost item. Again, drive was taken from the gearbox, but this time it was conveyed to a secondary gearbox that was mounted on the rear cross-member. The power could be taken direct from the splined end of the shaft, or transferred to a drum-type pulley suited to the wide belt drives typically used with farm machinery.

Vee belt drive from centre power take-off.

View showing cradles for carrying gas bottles.

WITH each Land-Rover mobile welding plant the following welding accessories are supplied, providing everything required to commence arc welding immediately.

1–30 foot length ground cable, with lugs. Lincoln flexible cable.

1–30 foot length electrode cable, Lincoln 'Stable Arc', extremely flexible with lug.

1 – Lincoln electrode holder, fitted to electrode cable.

1 – Lincoln ground clamp, fitted to ground cable.

1–Face shield, complete with standard visibility protective lens and non-spatter cover glass.

1–Wire scratch brush.

1–Chipping hammer.

## £825

*EXCLUSIVE OF GAS WELDING EQUIPMENT*

E. & O.E. Subject to alteration without notice.

View of arc welder showing control knobs.

Oil cooler located in front of radiator.

*The welder was produced in conjunction with the Lincoln Arc Welding Company, and came with everything that could reasonably be required to perform its job. However, individuals no doubt requested alterations or made some themselves. The welder undoubtedly contributed to Rover's eventual realisation that the fitting-out of specialist vehicles was best left to specialists.*

ear view showing generator and cables with gas bottles in position.

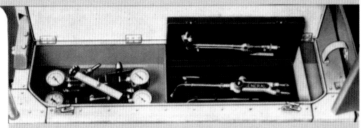

Cabinet at side of body containing welding equipment.

Cabinet housing nozzles, gauges and other equipment.

Land-Rover engine showing engine governor.

It was Alfred Bullows who provided the equipment for the compressor derivative of the Land Rover. The compressor was driven from the centre power take-off, but was otherwise a free-standing unit bolted to a bed-plate and secured by brackets around the rear chassis, so it did not justify a chassis number sequence of its own like the welder had.

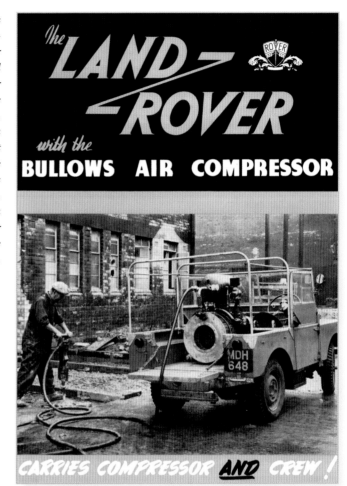

The LAND-ROVER with the BULLOWS AIR COMPRESSOR

CARRIES COMPRESSOR AND CREW!

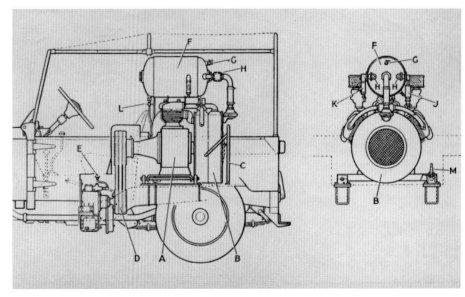

A—Compressor unit.
B—Cooler.
C—Cooler guard.
D—" V " belt drive.

E—Power take-off control lever.
F—Air receiver.
G—One ¾" B.S.P. outlet.
H—Two ¾" B.S.P. outlet valves.

J—Automatic unloader.
K—Safety valve.
L—Drain cock.
M—Drive belt adjuster.

The purpose-built Brockhouse trailer was capable of carrying 15cwt (762kg), and that effectively doubled the load capacity of the Land Rover. The trailers were designed to suit the original 80-inch model, but there were only minor modifications over the years. Sales continued in a somewhat desultory fashion right through until 1965.

A Capstan Winch designed to operate from the front of the Land-Rover. It is power driven from the front end of the engine crankshaft via a dog clutch and universal shaft. In conjunction with the sturdy Land-Rover it will be found of inestimable use in many ways for Farm and Forestry work and in Industry.

To the rear power take-off present from the days of the Centre-Steer and the centre power take-off available from the start of production, Land Rover added a third power take-off. This was at the front, and used a dog clutch on the nose of the engine crankshaft. Typically, it was used to drive a winch, and the winch that Land Rover made available was a capstan type. This advertising leaflet is dated October 1950, and the Land Rover visible behind the winch has the latest style of grille with circular cut-outs for the headlamps, introduced for the 1951 model-year.

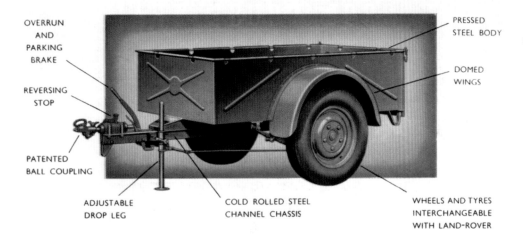

OVERRUN
AND
PARKING
BRAKE

REVERSING
STOP

PATENTED
BALL COUPLING

ADJUSTABLE
DROP LEG

COLD ROLLED STEEL
CHANNEL CHASSIS

PRESSED
STEEL BODY

DOMED
WINGS

WHEELS AND TYRES
INTERCHANGEABLE
WITH LAND-ROVER

## The LAND-ROVER
### SHOWING REAR SEATING

THESE removable seats will be found particularly useful when fitted to a Land-Rover having a metal detachable top, for converting it into an all enclosed weatherproof passenger carrying vehicle.

IN order to increase the usefulness of the Land-Rover two removable seats can be supplied for easy fitting in the rear of the body providing ample accommodation for four passengers. When not required for use the seat can be folded against the backrest allowing easy access and more space for the carriage of goods. When fitting the rear seats it is necessary to remove the spare wheel from the body, it is then carried in the alternative position on the top of the bonnet for which purpose a special fitting is supplied having clips which hold the wheel securely. When ordering rear seats the special wheel fitting should also be specified.

*Inward-facing bench seats in the rear had been fitted to the Land Rover presented to King George VI in July 1948, and they were welcomed by military users as well. However, they seem not to have been available to the general public before August 1949 – and then only on Export models. This leaflet advertising their availability was issued in March 1951.*

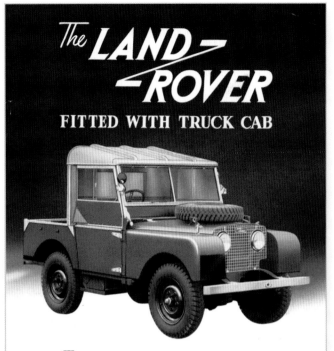

## The LAND-ROVER
### FITTED WITH TRUCK CAB

THE metal cab has been primarily designed for converting the Land-Rover into a small pick-up truck, when the Metal Detachable Top (E.7) would be an encumbrance to loading and discharging a vehicle principally engaged in light transport operations. This type of cab may also be fitted when it is desired to give to the driving compartment, a more weatherproof protection than that offered by the canvas hood.

*The aluminium-alloy truck cab was a particularly welcome addition in temperate climates. Introduced in October 1950, it was far more successful at keeping out the worst of the weather than the original "three-seater" hood, a canvas cover for the cab area only. It was always painted cream, as a way of reflecting heat in tropical climates. This sales leaflet dates from June 1952; just over a year later, the truck cab would become standard wear on the new 86-inch and 107-inch models for the UK.*

The cab is constructed of aluminium alloy, which in addition to being non-corrosive, assists, by its lightness, in maintaining the low centre of gravity of the Land-Rover.

The unit is secured to the Land-Rover by means of two clamps in the forward hood stick sockets, and at the top of the windscreen, through the two front hood stay bracket nuts. It is therefore easily and quickly removable. Rubber strip seals are fitted between the leading edge of the roof and the windscreen, and at the base of the rear panel, where this fits against the truck capping, thus effecting insulation against vibration and contributing to dust and draught sealing.

A sliding rear window of perspex fitted in the back panel affords excellent rear vision to the driver. The cab is painted overall in cream, to assist the interior cooling of the driving compartment when the Land-Rover is being used in hot climates.

# SELLING

The Land Rover was not like most other vehicles, and Rover faced a major task in creating public awareness of what, to most potential buyers, was something completely new on the market. To that end, they drew up suitable advertisements for their dealers to use in such local newspapers and magazines as they saw fit. The company published leaflets that illustrated the advertisements avail-able, and their dealers would make a choice from these.

Choice made, the dealer would contact Rover and request a copper printing block of the relevant advertisement. This would come with a space into which the dealer could insert his own contact details. The block would then be handed over to the relevant publication for printing. Some of these original blocks have survived to the present.

*These "generic" Land Rover advertisement blocks were avail-able in March 1950. The top three all show RHD models (where only a driver's windscreen wiper is present, it is on the right-hand side), with the then-current specification. The seat-backs are the "spade" type, which were sprung against the transom panel. At the bottom is the distinctive Land Rover logo.*

*Legend has it that this was inspired by the way a member of the Drawing Office used to sign his name, with a linking Z-shaped bar. Also legendary, but just as likely to be true, is that the oval in which the logo was usually seen came from the shape of the sardine tin in which he carried an element of his lunch.*

Matrices for the above blocks can be supplied separately in any size to order.

## Advertisement No. 2A

# Here is the LAND-ROVER
# ...with its
# 101 Industrial uses

The versatility of the Land-Rover is really amazing. A four-wheel drive towing and delivery wagon, a mobile power plant, and a fast economical vehicle on the road—the Land-Rover is all these things rolled into one. A fast, powerful, adaptable utility vehicle, it does a hundred-and-one useful jobs in industry. Built for hard work and hard wear it is supplied with right- or left-hand drive as required.

**Britain's most versatile vehicle**

DEALER'S NAME AND ADDRESS

*Made by the Rover Company Limited, Solihull, Birmingham, England*

*Rover were still thinking largely in terms of two groups of Land Rover users. One was farmers, and the other was those who worked in light industry. There was a third group – military users – but these were not influenced by public advertising. These three advertisements from 1950 were aimed at potential customers in industry.*

## Advertisement No. 23

# LAND-ROVER
## Britain's most versatile vehicle

### The 4-wheel drive all-purpose vehicle

The Land-Rover does more jobs than any other vehicle of its size. Towing heavy weights up slippery slopes, its low gearing and 4-wheel drive give it an octopus grip with a tug like a team of elephants. The power take-off can be coupled to anything that needs belt or shaft drive — pumps, compressors, generators, buzz saws, etc. It's designed for jobs no other vehicle can tackle . . . . . . . . and how well it does them !

DEALER'S

NAME AND ADDRESS

**MADE BY THE ROVER CO. LTD., SOLIHULL, BIRMINGHAM, ENGLAND**

CVS-45

## Advertisement No. 18

# Working for Prosperity-

## with the help of the LAND-ROVER

And what a help it is! Built for versatility this tough and compact little fellow is a four-wheel drive tractor, a delivery or towing wagon, a mobile power plant, and a fast, economical vehicle on the road. Whatever the job — it's as good as done when the Land-Rover's around. Supplied with left or right-hand drive as required.

# Britain's most versatile vehicle

### DEALER'S NAME AND ADDRESS

THE ROVER CO. LTD · SOLIHULL · BIRMINGHAM · ENGLAND

---

## Advertisement No. 22

# Wherever there's work to be done you'll find the LAND-ROVER

## WORKING FOR PROSPERITY

EARLY MORNING : the Land-Rover collects the milk, and comes back perhaps with a load of cattle feed from the Town. Next, to the wood where they're cutting timber ; the power take-off, coupled to the circular saw makes short work of a long job, and the four-wheel drive takes it over any sort of country. In the afternoon she's off to town again with a load of potatoes . . . the Land-Rover certainly earns its keep on the farm.

### DEALER'S NAME AND ADDRESS

MADE BY THE ROVER CO. LTD., SOLIHULL, BIRMINGHAM, ENGLAND

CVS-36

Advertisement No. 19A

# GO anywhere ... DO anything

The versatility of the Land-Rover is really amazing. A four-wheel drive tractor, a delivery wagon, a mobile power plant and a fast, economical vehicle on the road—the Land-Rover is all these things rolled into one. It is the ideal maid-of-all-work for farms or factories, and is supplied with right- or left-hand drive as required.

DEALER'S NAME AND ADDRESS

Britain's most versatile vehicle

**LAND ROVER**

*Made by the Rover Company Limited*
*Solihull, Birmingham, England*

Advertisement No. 20   4 x 3¾

# It's a fine job of work!

THE **LAND ROVER**

BUILT for toughness and versatility this compact little vehicle is a four-wheel drive tractor, a delivery wagon, a mobile power plant, and a fast economical vehicle on the road. There is no end to the jobs which can be done—quicker and easier — when the Land-Rover is around.

DEALER'S NAME AND ADDRESS

*Britain's most versatile vehicle*

MADE BY THE ROVER CO. LTD · SOLIHULL · BIRMINGHAM · ENGLAND

Advertisement No. 27

The Land-Rover is a thorough all-rounder. With its four-wheel drive and power take-off (belt or shaft drive) it can do things that many a larger vehicle would jib at. In industry and agriculture its applications are numerous ; as a runabout, as a towing vehicle and as a mobile power plant. The four-speed gear box, in conjunction with the transfer gear box gives eight forward speeds and two reverse. On the road or over rough country, on steep gradients and under heavy loads the Land-Rover earns its reputation as—

## Britain's most versatile vehicle

DEALER'S

NAME AND ADDRESS

MADE BY THE ROVER CO. LTD., SOLIHULL, BIRMINGHAM, ENGLAND

CVS-52

*"Working for prosperity" was a slogan of the times, inspired by the Ministry of Supply and the government's drive to haul Britain out of the economic doldrums where the 1939-1945 war had left it. It was particularly associated with farming, and these advertisements were both aimed at farmers. Again, they date from 1950.*

*The dealer who wanted to target a broader audience could choose from advertisements like these in 1950. They stressed the Land Rover's versatility. Although the picture showing goods being loaded at the docks was a new angle on the subject, the one with the sacks was almost certainly inspired by a photograph of the Centre-Steer dating from early 1948.*

## LAND ROVER

**STANDARD EQUIPMENT SUPPLIED WITH EACH VEHICLE**

Two aluminium doors with Perspex sidescreens
Full hood with rear panel
Cushions and back-rests for two front seat passengers
Spare wheel and tyre, 6·00" × 16"
Starting handle
Towing plate for rear draw bar
Pintle hook
Socket for trailer light
Hand rail

### £540

OTHER ITEMS OF EXTRA EQUIPMENT
AVAILABLE IF REQUIRED AS DETAILED
IN LIST BELOW

| | | £ s. d. |
|---|---|---|
| E/2 | Rear Power Take-off. Drive Section ... ... | 20 0 0 |
| E/3 | Rear Power Take-off. Pulley Unit ... ... | 15 0 0 |
| E/4 | Centre Power Take-off ... ... ... | 7 0 0 |
| E/6a | Pulley and Fitting for E/4 ... ... ... | 2 10 0 |
| E/6b | Pulley and Fitting for E/4 where used in conjunction with E/2 ... ... ... ... | 2 10 0 |
| E/11 | Rear Winch (E/2 must be specified also) ... | 26 0 0 |
| E/5 | Engine Governor Unit ... ... ... ... | 15 0 0 |
| E/31 | Oil Cooler Unit (Not supplied without E/34) ... | Price to be announced |
| E/34 | 15-lb. Pressure Radiator Cap. Essential with E/31 | ,, |
| E/12 | Thermometer and Oil Gauge ... ... ... | ,, |
| E/8 | Five detachable rim wheels in place of five standard wheels ... ... ... ... | 8 14 6 |
| E/9 | Extra for five 7.00" × 16" Dunlop Tractor Tread Tyres instead of standard 6.00" × 16" Tyres | 10 10 0 |

P.T.O.

## LAND ROVER

*List of extras continued*

| | | £ s. d. |
|---|---|---|
| E/35 | Extra for five 7.00" × 16" Dunlop "Fort" Tyres instead of Standard 6.00" × 16" Tyres ... | 10 10 0 |
| E/15a | Carrier on bonnet for 6.00" × 16" Tyres ... | 1 0 0 |
| E/15b | Carrier on bonnet for 7.00" × 16" Tyres ... | 1 0 0 |
| E/10 | Chaff Guard ... ... ... ... | 2 0 0 |
| E/18 | Ventilator for Windscreen ... ... ... | 1 15 0 |
| E/7a | Detachable metal top covering Driver's and rear compartments ... ... ... | See separate leaflet |
| E/14 | Electric Heater ... ... ... ... | 7 0 0 |
| E/23 | Trafficators ... ... ... ... | 3 2 6 |
| E/28 | Heavy Duty Army Type Pintle Hook ... ... | 1 10 0 |
| E/25 | Grass Shield for Universal Joints ... | Price on application |
| E/27 | Brockhouse 15 cwt. Trailer ... ... (For description see separate leaflet) | 75 0 0 |

### NOTES

The Engine Governor E/5 is essential if the Centre Power Take-off is specified, or if a Rear Power Take-off is specified with Pulley Unit E/3.

If both Rear and Centre Power Take-off are specified pulley and fittings E/6b must be supplied.

The prices quoted for extra equipment are valid only if such extra equipment is fitted before vehicle is delivered from Works. If ordered after delivery from Works a fitting charge will be made. All prices and specifications quoted in this catalogue of which this leaflet forms a part are subject to alteration without notice. Prices are for delivery ex Works.

No allowance can be made in respect of any item of Standard Equipment not required.

The Land-Rover is subject to the guarantee conditions contained in The Guarantee Form issued by The Rover Company Limited.

The name "Land-Rover" is a registered Trade Mark of The Rover Company Ltd.

E. & O. E.                                          July/50.

---

## LAND ROVER

### 4 - WHEEL DRIVE PICK - UP

**STANDARD EQUIPMENT SUPPLIED
WITH EACH VEHICLE**

Two doors with Perspex sidescreens; detachable metal truck cab with sliding rear window; cushions and back-rests for two passengers; spare wheel and tyre, 7.00" × 16"; starting handle; driving mirror; towing plate for rear draw bar; pintle hook.

### PRICES

| | | £ s. d. |
|---|---|---|
| STANDARD MODEL | ... ... | £635 0 0 |
| DE LUXE MODEL | ... ... | £655 0 0 |

Subject to alteration without notice.

SEPT., 1953

*Early Land Rover price lists rarely survive; they lack the appeal that persuades people to keep the illustrated sales catalogues. However, this one has survived and reveals what Land Rover buyers in the UK were paying in July 1950. The list of E-coded options (the E probably stood for nothing more exciting than Extra) would reach several thousand by the end of the period covered by this book.*

*This is another welcome survivor, and slips of paper like this were often pinned inside the sales catalogues by dealer staff. The standard specification now includes much more than before – notably a truck cab – and the cost has risen to reflect that. The list dates from September 1953 and is actually for a 107-inch model.*

# EXPORT – THE NAME OF THE GAME

If it hadn't been for the British Government's demand for exports above all else in the late 1940s, there would probably never have been a Land Rover at all. So export became the name of the game very early on in the model's history. Right from the very start, the orders poured in – and not just for individual vehicles but for large fleet batches as well. By 1950, the Land Rover was selling twice as well as the cars from which Rover had made its name, and it was obvious that the company had a viable long-term product on its hands.

Exports of fully-assembled vehicles were followed from 1950 by exports of CKD (Completely Knocked Down) models – kits of parts that could be assembled in the destination country, so providing work for the local workforce and also avoiding punitive import taxes. Overall, exports rapidly began to account for the lion's share of all the Land Rovers built, and that situation has continued up to the present. The exact figures have varied over the years, but a typical annual figure for Land Rover exports was 70% of production, including CKD.

Usually, it was overseas taxes that caused problems for the Rover Company, but there was one notable case where it was taxes at home that caused a problem. This involved the first Land Rover Station Wagon.

Rover's Maurice Wilks was convinced that there was a market for a passenger-carrying variant of the Land Rover, and he initially imagined that such a model might appeal to the landed gentry in Britain – those who owned large shooting estates in Scotland, for example, and who needed to ferry shooting parties around the rugged terrain of those estates. Other potential customers were hotel owners who needed a small bus to collect guests from the nearby station or airport. Influenced by the model that Jeep were building in the USA on their long-wheelbase chassis, he chose the name Station Wagon for the Land Rover variant, even though Estate Car or Shooting Brake would have been more familiar terms in late 1940s Britain.

"Meets every occasion"

Inevitably, this was going to be a smaller-volume model than the mainstream Land Rover, and Rover decided to farm the production of its body out to a specialist company. They had done exactly the same before the war when they had wanted small numbers of drophead coupé bodies on the chassis they otherwise built up as saloons. They even turned

*Justifying the model's name and illustrating one of its uses, this was the cover of the Station Wagon sales brochure. As so often happens, however, the reality was somewhat different from what was illustrated. The vehicle pictured was actually the prototype, and that finish featuring contrasting paint on the body side pressings was used only for the first handful of production vehicles. The prototype also had a divided windscreen, which was replaced on production models by a single-pane type. The vehicle's registration number was not GWD 252, either ...*

*This was the original picture on which the sales brochure was based. It was taken at Olton station, near Solihull. The artist's airbrush has filled in a great deal of detail that was not present here, in particular the station roof (where some damage has been made good, too) and the arrival of a smiling porter in place of the two rather sheepish-looking individuals in the photograph.*

to the same company to do the job – Salmons-Tickford of Newport Pagnell. The "Tickford" Station Wagon body was quite different from the standard Land Rover type, being constructed as a typical coachbuilt structure with aluminium panels attached to a wooden frame. It was built by hand, and was therefore expensive – and that was reflected in the showroom price.

Two problems arose. The first was that Land Rover sales were primarily geared to export markets, and that the wooden body frames did not hold up well on the rough roads of many overseas territories where they found buyers. The other was that the Station Wagon was a passenger-carrying vehicle, and was therefore subject to Purchase Tax in the UK, whereas the standard Land Rover was a commercial vehicle and was therefore exempted from this tax. That made the model formidably expensive in its home country, and was a major deterrent to sales. By 1951, it was clear that sales were always going to be slow both at home and abroad, and so the model was withdrawn.

*Another picture of the prototype was used inside the brochure, because no production example had been built, let alone photographed, by the time the brochure went to print in October 1948. The first production models were not built until March 1949.*

THE "Go anywhere" VEHICLE

*It's a right-hand drive Land Rover, but the significance of its position on top of a globe in this illustration from a 1952 catalogue was twofold. On the one hand, the Land Rover was already bestriding the globe thanks to booming exports. Figuratively speaking, it was on top of the world, too.*

4 WHEEL DRIVE. GOES *Anywhere*

*The Station Wagon was expensive enough before tax: a standard Land Rover cost just £540, so this was nearly 40% more. The killer was that Purchase Tax, which made the Station Wagon a luxury purchase. In the April 1951 Budget, Purchase Tax was doubled on cars with a base cost of £1000 or more, and no doubt Rover could see that the Station Wagon might reach that ceiling before too long in a climate where the cost of raw materials was on the increase.*

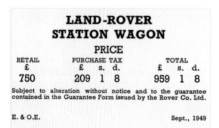

**LAND-ROVER STATION WAGON**

PRICE

| RETAIL £ | PURCHASE TAX £ s. d. | TOTAL £ s. d. |
|---|---|---|
| 750 | 209 1 8 | 959 1 8 |

Subject to alteration without notice and to the guarantee contained in the Guarantee Form issued by the Rover Co. Ltd.

E. & O.E.                           Sept., 1949

*Advertisement blocks were in English, but Rover had to start coping with foreign languages as well – and not just those found in Europe. This driver's handbook was prepared for customers in Korea.*

1951~1953

LAND-ROVER

ランドロバー解説書

東京都千代田区永田町交丁目八十六番地
朝日自動車株式會社
電話番号(58) 0716, 0717, 1608, 1609

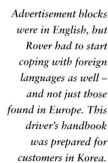

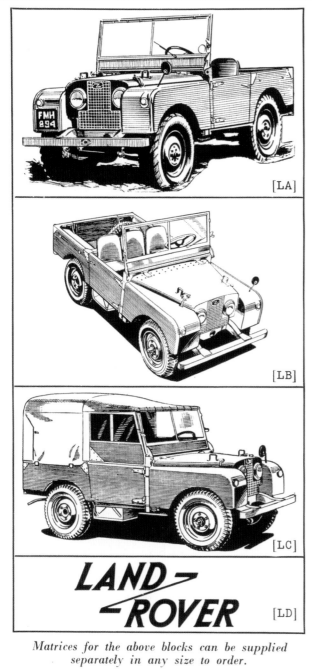

[LA]

[LB]

[LC]

LAND ROVER [LD]

*Matrices for the above blocks can be supplied separately in any size to order.*

Advertisement No. 37

★ 50 B.H.P. ENGINE
★ 4 WHEEL DRIVE
★ 8 FORWARD & 2 REVERSE GEARS

...AND
*Detachable*
METAL TOP

LAND ROVER **is built for hard work**

*This shows the detachable top lifted clear of the body. The change can be made in a few minutes, the top being secured by four bolts and wing-nuts.*

There is always work for the Land-Rover. It gives day-in, day-out, round the clock service. It is designed to perform those extraordinary jobs that are outside the capacity of a more conventional vehicle; with the four-wheel-drive in operation it will go anywhere through mud, sand, over ploughed fields and ditches. The lightweight detachable metal top is strongly built and fits closely to the top of the body; at the same time it is easily removable. Considerable attention has been given to eliminating the entry of dust.

DEALER'S
NAME AND ADDRESS

MADE BY THE ROVER COMPANY, LIMITED, SOLIHULL, BIRMINGHAM, ENGLAND

*By Appointment to the late King George VI*
*Land-Rover Manufacturers*

CVS

It was no use advertising Land Rovers in the local newspapers and magazines with pictures of right-hand drive models if the local preference was for the steering wheel on the left. So by 1952, when these advertisement blocks were drawn up, Rover had instructed their artists to show the vehicles as most export buyers wanted them.

*Handleiding,*

MINERVA
*Licence Rover*

Rover's Belgian agents managed to secure a large fleet order from the local military authorities in the early 1950s, but a condition of the deal was that the vehicles had a high degree of local content. So Belgian car maker Minerva set up an assembly operation, making the body-work of steel rather than aluminium. The Minerva Land Rovers featured special angular front wings. This was the special handbook, in Flemish on this side but in French if turned over and read from the back.

*Korean customers had to put up with the British sense of humour. Illustrations like these – uncredited, but certainly in the style of the British motoring cartoonist Russell Brockbank – were inserted into the text at intervals. The first one makes the point that the radiator cap should not be removed when the engine is hot. The second seems to encourage owners to examine components carefully before buying replacements, and the third reminds them that the registration number is no use at all when corresponding with the factory's service department; what is needed is the chassis number.*

先づヒューズを調べる

登録番号は役に立ちません

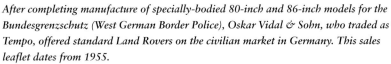

After completing manufacture of specially-bodied 80-inch and 86-inch models for the Bundesgrenzschutz (West German Border Police), Oskar Vidal & Sohn, who traded as Tempo, offered standard Land Rovers on the civilian market in Germany. This sales leaflet dates from 1955.

Cold winters in Sweden demanded better weatherproofing and heating arrangements than came as standard on Land Rovers. The Swedish importers, Wiklunds, were permitted to commission special weatherproof cabs with heavy-duty heaters, and they had this built by Grantorpets AG in Sweden. Grantorpets were better known under their trade name of Gripkarosserier AB (more familiarly, Grip). This advertisement shows both the special cab on an 86-inch in use as a snow plough, and a very special station wagon also built by Grip.

*The Grip cab was not only wider but also longer than standard. So the load bed was moved backwards to make room for it, giving a longer than standard rear overhang.*

*The Station Wagon was very special indeed. Not only did it have a coachbuilt body that was designed to keep out the worst of the Swedish weather, but it also had a chassis extension. The first ones added 40cm (15.7 inches) to an 80-inch chassis; later models achieved the same overall length by extending an 86-inch chassis.*

# RED ALERT

The Land Rover was an obvious choice as a rural or factory fire engine. Small, nimble and capable of crossing terrain that would stop other vehicles, it needed only to carry a ladder and extinguishers to serve as a first-aid vehicle until the full-size appliances arrived. As early as 1948, examples were bought by rural brigades in Portugal and kitted out for the purpose; in the UK, the Derby brigade did the same in 1949.

Land Rover recognised the potential, and planned to go one better with a factory-built model. One of the pre-production models was converted to a fire engine, complete with a first-aid water tank in the load bed, a hose reel mounted on top of that, and a rear-mounted fire pump driven from the centre power take-off. It also had a ladder rack and a searchlight.

However, getting a fire engine version of the Land Rover into production took some time, and it was not until May 1952 that it appeared. By this time, the original 1.6-litre engine in all models had been uprated to 2.0 litres, with no

*The truck cab was an extra-cost option for the fire engine, just as for the ordinary Land Rover. The spare wheel had to go in its optional position on the bonnet to make room for the first-aid tank in the rear, and the fire pump was supplied by specialists Pegson. The larger hoses could be carried on the front of the vehicle in a special cradle; the ladder rack is not shown here. Noteworthy here is that the vehicle is fitted with road tyres rather than the dual-purpose types that were standard equipment on other Land Rovers. The external handle on the door and the new grille with its inverted T-shape had both appeared for the first time on 1952-model Land Rovers, along with the 2.0-litre engine.*

*Colour photography was still expensive in 1952, but black-and-white pictures could be hand-tinted. This one was. The original seems to have been one of several taken next to a river, which provided the water for the fire pump as well as the target for the hoses. The river has disappeared here, though, and there are ominous-looking clouds of back smoke tinged with red to suggest the fire that is being tackled.*

extra power but welcome additional torque. All the Land Rover fire engines were delivered painted red, with red seats and wheels, and even a red chassis.

A difficulty then arose. Rover had been counting on their standard specification having universal appeal, but many customers began to request special features. The ideal configuration for a factory fire engine, for example, was not the same as that required for forestry protection work; and individual chief fire officers all tended to have their own favourite equipment suppliers as well. Overseas customers sometimes requested different hose couplings from the British type to suit their local standards. This made building fire engines on the lines next to impossible, and by 1955 the whole business had been transferred to the Technical Sales Department, which also looked after requests for other special equipment. Rover must have breathed a sigh of relief in 1959 when they were able to hand over fire engine production to specialists such as Carmichael's of Worcester.

THE
**LAND ROVER**
FIRE ENGINE

PRICE.... .... .... .... .... £905   0   0

METAL DETACHABLE CAB
available as an optional extra   .... £25  11   0

ALL VEHICLES ARE SOLD SUBJECT TO PRICE CURRENT
AT TIME OF DELIVERY.

MAY, 1953

*Typically, the price of a fire engine was to be found on a little slip of paper tucked inside the sales catalogue or pinned to it. This one dates from May 1953.*

*The* **LAND ROVER**

**FIRE ENGINE**

*The design of the fire engine was gradually refined and improved, and those built on the 86-inch chassis that replaced the original 80-inch type in autumn 1953 were even better equipped. Customers had requested equipment lockers, and these were fitted in the sides of the newly elongated load-bed, with canvas covers. The example pictured for the catalogue cover did not have the truck cab which was almost universal on UK-market vehicles by this time, and nor did it have the ladder-rack that so many brigades fitted.*

31

The 86-inch fire engine used a German-made KSB fire pump instead of the earlier Pegson type, and the control panel was different, too. This vehicle shows the recessed door handles introduced on all 1954-model Land Rovers, but is clearly a 1955 model because it has the "pork-pie" tail lamps introduced for that model-year.

This was the configuration available for British buyers, with the truck cab usually fitted as protection against the notoriously fickle British climate. There was a certain rightness about this configuration which is hard to explain but nevertheless obvious from the pictures.

# BIGGER AND BETTER

Right from the start, users had over-loaded their Land Rovers, and it became clear at Solihull that one of their vehicle's main failings was that it was too small. First they came up with a matching trailer as an extra-cost accessory, but what was really needed was a bigger load bed. This became doubly obvious when the military tried to squeeze four soldiers and full kit into the back of an 80-inch, and as the military were such good customers, Rover decided something had to be done.

In fact, they dealt with the problem in two ways. They enlarged the load-bed of the existing Land Rover by adding six inches to the wheelbase and a further three inches of over-hang at the rear. This gave a 25% increase in carrying capacity, and allowed those uncomfortable soldiers to breathe more easily. They also designed an addition to the Land Rover range. This had an extra 27 inches in the wheelbase, the lengthened rear overhang, and a load-bed that was a full six feet long. It was designed as a pick-up truck, and was initially called exactly that, although over time the two new models, both introduced in October 1953, became known as 86-inch and 107-inch types.

The original Land Rover Station Wagon had gone out of production in 1951, but there was still a market for such a vehicle. So Rover put together a Station Wagon derivative of the 86-inch model, using mainly optional extras already available and adding a few other items to complete the package. This kept the manufacturing cost and therefore the purchase price at sensible levels, and the seven-seat Station Wagon became a popular model.

So well was the 86-inch Station Wagon received that Rover soon began to look at creating a similar vehicle on the 107-inch chassis. Unfortunately, there were problems. The upswept side members of the 107-inch chassis did not allow the flat floor needed for a Station Wagon, and so the side members had to be redesigned. At the same time, the rear springs were mounted on outriggers instead of directly to the side members, to reduce roll when the vehicle was fully laden with the ten passengers it was designed to carry. Rover could not get the redesigned chassis into production until June 1956 – by which time the mainstream models were just about to be updated with another change of wheelbase. So the 107 Station Wagon was an anomaly in the range from its arrival until its demise in mid-1958.

*"Now bigger and better," they said, although the artist has perhaps gone a little too far in suggesting the extended rear overhang of the 86-inch model for this 1954-season catalogue. The 86-inch and 107-inch models were not promoted in the same catalogues at this stage, because they were seen as quite separate models.*

*This was what the changes in wheelbase for the 1954 model-year were all about – creating more carrying capacity in the Land Rover. This illustration from a 1955 catalogue shows how it had been achieved, and what a big difference it made.*

THE 86in. WHEELBASE LAND-ROVER GIVES 25% MORE CAPACITY

*The above illustration shows graphically just what the 6-inch extension in the Land-Rover wheelbase means. The rear load-carrying section is extended by 9 inches, giving a 25% increase in carrying capacity and more space for bulky loads. In addition, riding and road-holding qualities—always outstanding—are now even better.*

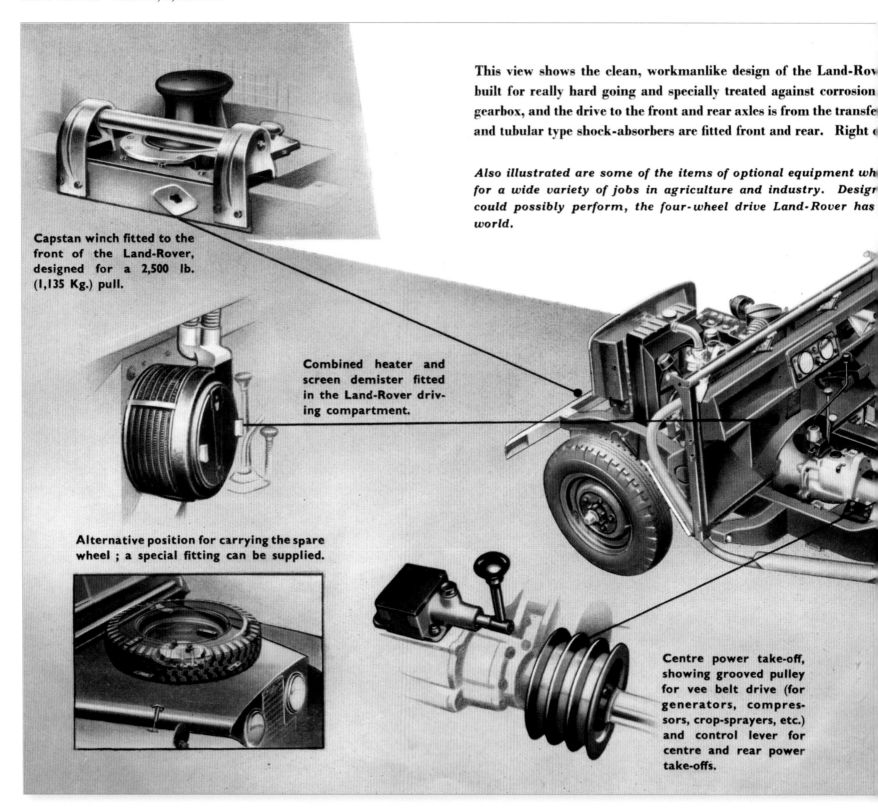

This view shows the clean, workmanlike design of the Land-Rov
built for really hard going and specially treated against corrosion
gearbox, and the drive to the front and rear axles is from the transfe
and tubular type shock-absorbers are fitted front and rear.   Right

*Also illustrated are some of the items of optional equipment wh
for a wide variety of jobs in agriculture and industry.   Desigr
could possibly perform, the four-wheel drive Land-Rover has
world.*

**Capstan winch fitted to the front of the Land-Rover, designed for a 2,500 lb. (1,135 Kg.) pull.**

**Combined heater and screen demister fitted in the Land-Rover driving compartment.**

**Alternative position for carrying the spare wheel ; a special fitting can be supplied.**

**Centre power take-off, showing grooved pulley for vee belt drive (for generators, compressors, crop-sprayers, etc.) and control lever for centre and rear power take-offs.**

*As before, there was a range of extra-cost options for the 1954 Land Rovers. The overall design of the chassis was just as it had been before, too, despite the extra length.*

...sis, and illustrates the immensely rigid box section chassis frame—
...rive for centre and rear power take-offs is taken through the main
...The suspension system is capable of dealing with the roughest ground,
...and steering can be fitted as required.

...ke the Land-Rover a highly mobile power-unit, eminently suitable
...perate in all conditions, built for work that no ordinary vehicle
...y proved itself invaluable for every kind of task throughout the

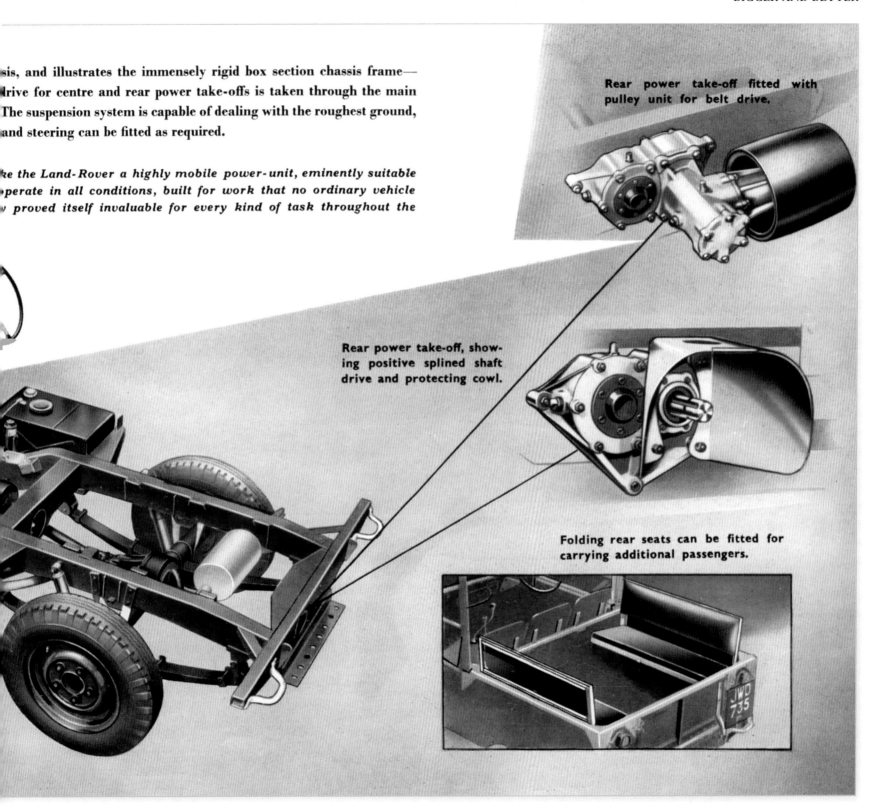

**Rear power take-off fitted with pulley unit for belt drive.**

**Rear power take-off, showing positive splined shaft drive and protecting cowl.**

**Folding rear seats can be fitted for carrying additional passengers.**

*The picture at bottom right illustrating the optional rear seats almost certainly shows an 80-inch model (that registration number was issued in 1950, and this is a retouched photograph), but it is highly unlikely that anybody noticed the shorter back body!*

This was the standard configuration in most markets. The 86-inch model came with a removable canvas top that covered both driving compartment and load area. It was not the same colour as the bodywork, even though this retouched picture suggests that it was; the colour was actually khaki. In fact, new colour options had arrived with the 1954 models, and instead of the Bronze Green that had earlier been ubiquitous, buyers could now order their Land Rovers in blue or grey. These had their own complementary soft top colours.

The Land-Rover in open trim, with canvas hood, hood-sticks and side-screens removed. The windscreen can be folded flat.

The Land-Rover with canvas hood and side-screens in position.

The three illustrations to the right are from the 1954 sales catalogue and were intended to show some of the Land Rover's uses on the farm. All of them were re-touched photographs, and pictured to the left is the original of the first illustration. DPR 42 was actually a 1949 80-inch that belonged to the Hibberd family who farmed at Cranborne in Dorset. In the later 1950s, Stuart Hibberd used it very successfully in trials organised by the Land Rover Owners' Club.

The Land-Rover makes light work of a load like this, however tough the going may be.

The lightweight metal detachable top, showing method of removal and (inset) the lift-up rear door.

The Land-Rover fitted with the lightweight metal detachable top.

Re-touched photographs were still domi-nant in Land Rover sales catalogues, and it would have been very difficult to illustrate how the hardtop fitted to the body without the artist's skills on display here. The picture is actually of what Rover called a "window hardtop"; this was available for export markets but would have incurred Purchase Tax in the UK and was therefore not on offer. Home market customers could only have a hardtop with plain sides.

Operating a power-driven mower—one of the many uses of the rear power take-off.

Building, contracting, surveying — wherever there's a job of work to be done the Land-Rover will be there.

By 1955, Rover's main aim seemed to be demonstrating the Land Rover's world-wide success, and the cover of the catalogue for the 86-inch models set the tone by showing 86-inch models in quantity.

Here are more, lined up awaiting despatch to dealers. The building in the background is readily recognisable as the main office block at Rover's Solihull factory. It is still standing today. The cars parked outside (which would have belonged to the Rover Directors), are all Rover P4 models.

Not only in this country is the Land-Rover continually giving new demonstrations of its versatility and all-round usefulness; all over the world, in every climate and in all conditions, on roads which exist in name only or not at all, the Land-Rover is giving unrivalled service. Ever since it was first introduced, this unique all-purpose vehicle has been in world-wide demand—a demand which increases steadily and shows no sign of falling off. On the inside back cover of this catalogue you will find a list of some of the many government departments, industrial and other organisations and private individuals now using Land-Rovers. This is only a brief selection from a list which grows longer every day, an impressive record of the sales—and, by the same token, the multiplicity of uses—of a vehicle the name of which is rapidly becoming a by-word for tireless efficiency.

*Though the first flush of the British Government's drive to boost exports was over, Land Rover exports were still expanding in the mid-1950s. A Land Rover is seen here being swung aloft by a crane for loading aboard a cargo vessel that will take it to its new owners abroad. The scene is reasonably realistic, although it is doubtful whether Land Rovers were often lined up in such neat rows on the dockside!*

*Versatility as well as ubiquity … some of the pictures used here actually show 80-inch models, but they have been "re-arted" to pass muster as 86s. "The World's Most Versatile Vehicle" was a slogan that appeared over and over again in Land Rover promotional material.*

the many uses of

On the farm, in industry . . .

e work is hard and the going is tough,

there's a place for the indefatigable Land-Rover.

### REAR POWER TAKE-OFF
(with pulley unit)

**1** The rear power take-off is driven through the main shaft of the main gearbox, and with the pulley unit provides belt drive for circular saws, rick elevators and other belt-driven machinery

### REAR POWER TAKE-OFF
(with shaft drive)

**2** By removing four nuts only the pulley unit can be taken off, revealing a splined positive drive shaft suitable for operating hammer mills, mowers and other machinery requiring non-slip drive. A cowl is fitted for protection.

### CENTRE POWER TAKE-OFF

**3** Located at the forward end of the rear power take-off drive shaft, the centre power take-off is controlled by a lever and knob on top of the main gearbox. The driving pulley is grooved for V-belts, and will drive generators, sprayers and other machinery capable of being mounted in the vehicle.

### CENTRE POWER TAKE-OFF
(showing belt drive)

**4** This illustration shows the centre power take-off with three V-belts, driving a generator for a mobile arc welding plant. The centre seat cushion is removed, and the driving mechanism is covered by a cowl for protection. The control lever is on the right.

### HEATER AND DEMISTER

**5** Provision is made for the fitting of a heater coupled to the cooling system. Built into the heater is a fan which, when switched on, draws in cool air, heats it and passes it through two small adjustable doors into the body of the vehicle. Also available are demister nozzles of very effective power.

### ALTERNATIVE SPARE WHEEL CARRIER

**6** The standard carrying bracket for the spare wheel is behind the front seats, but an alternative position is provided on top of the bonnet, leaving the whole of the body carrying space free for extra-bulky loads. A special fitting can be supplied as an optional extra.

### FRONT CAPSTAN WINCH

**7** For moving heavy machinery, grubbing out old tree roots, etc., a power-driven front winch is available, mounted between the forward end of the chassis side members and the front bumper and driven from the front end of the crankshaft via a dog clutch and universal shaft. The winch is designed for a 2,500 lb. (1·135 Kg.) pull, and should be used with the engine running at a speed of 600 r.p.m. (i.e., fast idling speed). The ratio of the worm drive is 75 : 1, giving a rope speed of 9·6 ft. (2·9 m.) per minute at 600 r.p.m. A hand throttle control, also supplied as an optional extra, is advisable if the front winch is specified, as this enables engine revolutions to be kept below the recommended limit.

THE optional extras illustrated on these two pages are only a few of the many available and specially designed for use with the Land-Rover. In the back of this catalogue will be found a more comprehensive list of optional extras, with prices, and your local Distributor or Dealer will be glad to advise on their fitting and their various uses. In cases of difficulty the Technical Service Department of The Rover Company Limited will also be pleased to give advice on request.

*The major extras were the same as they had been for the later 80-inch models, but by the mid-1950s some aftermarket specialists had begun to develop special conversions for the Land Rover that would make it more versatile than ever. The Technical Sales Department, responsible for keeping an eye on such things and generally assisting customers who wanted a Land Rover to perform a special function, was soon overwhelmed.*

*This must be one of the best-loved of all images of the early Land Rover. The unknown artist excelled himself, depicting a well-laden 86-inch model kicking up the dust on a mountain road. NAC 750 really existed; it was the fifth prototype of the 86-inch Land Rover and, like all the first year's production models, it had the same D-shaped tail lamps as the superseded 80-inch type.*

*The Station Wagon roof was special: windows in its sides reduced the feeling of claustrophobia for those sitting in the inward-facing seats at the back, and also allowed the driver to see upwards out of the vehicle – useful on hairpin bends in mountainous regions like the Alps. The windows were known as Alpine lights in consequence. The second-skin or "tropical" roof allowed air to flow between the two roof panels, so reducing the temperature inside the passenger compartment.*

*By using readily-available production options and adding a few special features, Rover were able to create an affordable seven-seat Station Wagon on the 86-inch chassis. This is a French-market sales catalogue for the model. Behind the cover picture lies a story. "NAD 749" was actually NAC 749, and was the prototype 86-inch Station Wagon. The original photograph was taken at Olton Station, and at that stage the vehicle had side and rear windows that differed from one side to the other. The artist has airbrushed the differences out, and added in details such as the train – but a careful look at the tail window on the far side, visible through the vehicle, shows that it is not quite realistically placed.*

*Some time around 1955, the Rover Company commissioned a number of Land Rover paintings from Terence Cuneo, the great military and railway painter who was also the official artist for the 1953 Coronation of Queen Elizabeth II. This magnificent farmyard scene became the cover of a 1956-season catalogue. The artist's signature is visible at bottom right.*

*The Land Rover was never quite as successful on the farm as Maurice Wilks had originally imagined; farmers generally preferred to use tractors to drive farm machinery. So this picture of an 86 from the mid-1950s shows the reality. The Land Rover is being used as the farm runabout – a job at which it certainly did excel – and the hay baling machine is being driven by something else, out of shot.*

The 2.0-litre IOE petrol engine remained the standard Land Rover power plant until 1958. The artist has used a bit of licence here in his presentation of the engine, which was certainly never finished in yellow.

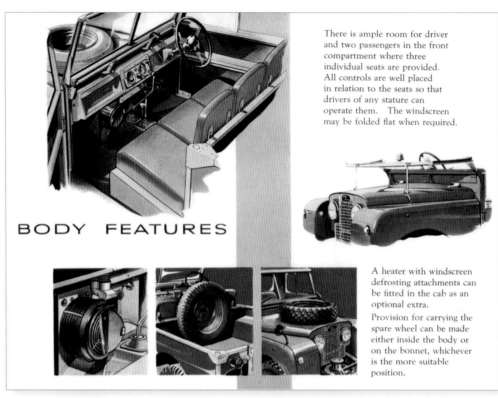

BODY FEATURES

There is ample room for driver and two passengers in the front compartment where three individual seats are provided. All controls are well placed in relation to the seats so that drivers of any stature can operate them. The windscreen may be folded flat when required.

A heater with windscreen defrosting attachments can be fitted in the cab as an optional extra.

Provision for carrying the spare wheel can be made either inside the body or on the bonnet, whichever is the more suitable position.

There is some artistic licence in the colours here, too, although the blue of the bodywork is reasonably representative of the actual colour available. The heater, made by Smith's, made quite a difference in cold weather, but was notorious for burning the passenger's legs while leaving the driver with cold feet.

The new 107-inch Land Rover was specifically designed as a pick-up truck, and was actually called that in some early publications issued when it was new in September 1953. However, before long it was being described as the Long Wheelbase model, and today it is generally described as a 107 to distinguish it from later long-wheelbase types. Early examples, as seen in the station scene, were in grey with a blue chassis and wheels or blue with a grey chassis and wheels – attractive but of little consequence to the model's buyers.

By the time of this illustration for a 1956 catalogue, the contrasting colours for chassis and wheels were no longer available.

For the 107, buyers could order a special De Luxe cab, which added floor coverings and door trims to the standard specification. The upholstery was in a new check-pattern vinyl for both standard and De Luxe types.

*This illustration shows the interior of the cab as fitted on the De Luxe model—revealing a high standard of comfort, finish and tasteful styling not usually found in a vehicle designed for slogging it out with the roughest going the world can offer. Right or left-hand drive can be supplied as required.*

In the early days of the 107, Rover believed they were tackling a new market – that for pick-up trucks – which was separate from the one they had already addressed. For potential buyers who had perhaps never considered a Land Rover because it had always been too small, the value of four-wheel drive needed to be explained.

Right from the start, the ten-seater Station Wagon was described as a 107-inch model. Perhaps the main reason was that by the time it was introduced, the other long-wheelbase models had become 109-inch types. The area around the rear doors always looked somewhat crude, as if it had been bolted together from a Meccano construction set. The front doors were shared with the short-wheelbase models, but the rear door needed its handle mounted higher up in order to clear the wheel arch. This beige colour, appropriately known as Sand, did become available for export models.

THE LAND-ROVER 107" STATION WAGON

## Land-Rover Long Station Wagon

Based on the 107-in. wheelbase chassis the Long Station Wagon is a ten-seater, go-anywhere personnel carrier.

The seating arrangement provides accommodation for three people in front, three on the back seat and four, facing inward, on additional seats fitted to the rear wheel boxes. If the wheel box seats are removed and the back seat is folded right forward the whole body is available for load carrying. Alternatively, the back seat squab can be folded backward and the front seat cushions and squab redisposed to form a comfortable bed.

As late as 1958, when this catalogue was issued, the illustration of the 107 Station Wagon's interior was misleading. The rear door window on production models was not rubber-glazed; this drawing had clearly been done from one of the prototypes, which did initially have rubber-glazed windows. The ten-seat capacity was achieved by seating three on each of the transverse bench seats, and two on each of the inward-facing benches in the rear.

LAND-ROVER **LONG STATION WAGON**

This was another classic Land Rover sales catalogue cover, showing a 107 Station Wagon out on the tarmac at an airport. The aircraft is a Vickers Viscount, a popular medium-range four-turboprop airliner of the 1950s. British European Airways became part of British Airways in 1974.

Rover promoted the 107 Station Wagon as a personnel carrier, but it also became much liked as an expedition vehicle. However, despite the flooring, door trims and even a headlining, it was still very much a commercial vehicle rather than the alternative to a conventional car that later models became.

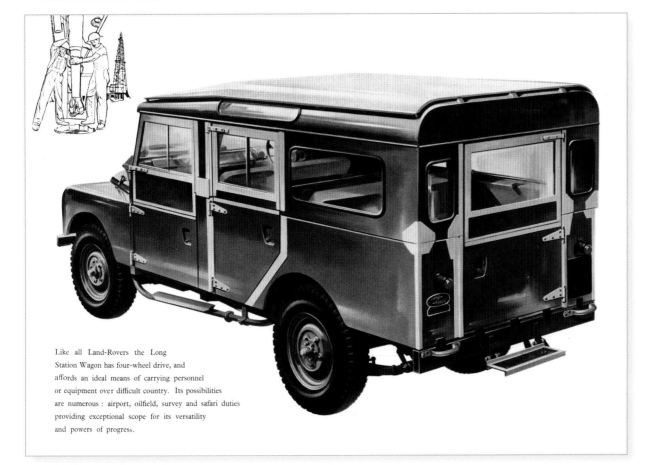

Like all Land-Rovers the Long Station Wagon has four-wheel drive, and affords an ideal means of carrying personnel or equipment over difficult country. Its possibilities are numerous : airport, oilfield, survey and safari duties providing exceptional scope for its versatility and powers of progress.

When the Series II models were introduced in 1958, all earlier Land Rovers automatically became Series I types, regardless of wheelbase. This was actually the factory's own designation, as the cover of this handbook shows.

INSTRUCTION MANUAL

PART No. 4277

LAND-ROVER

1948-58 SERIES I

# A DIESEL OPTION

The Land Rover had originally been powered by a petrol engine because Rover only had petrol engines in production when it was first produced. However, this was a commercial vehicle, and many of its buyers were fleet owners whose other vehicles were diesel-powered. Having a petrol-engined vehicle on such a fleet was a nuisance, and it was clear by about 1953 that the absence of a diesel option for the Land Rover was costing sales. One British company, Turner Engineering of Wolverhampton, developed a diesel conversion to meet the demand, using a Jenbach engine built in Austria.

Rover were well aware of the need for a diesel engine. When there were discussions between Rover and Standard in 1954 about the possibility of a merger, one of the interesting aspects for Rover was access to the 2.1-litre diesel engine that Standard were building for Ferguson tractors. It was the look of Standard's accounts that eventually put Rover off the idea of a merger, but the fact that its engineers had discovered the Standard engine would not fit into a

| | PRICE | Purchase Tax | TOTAL |
|---|---|---|---|
| | £ s. d. | £ s. d. | £ s. d. |
| **88 in. Wheelbase Vehicle** ... ... | 615 0 0 | — | |
| **Station Wagons:** | | | |
| 88 in. Wheelbase | 685 0 0 | 343 17 0 | 1028 17 0 |
| 107 in. Wheelbase | 790 0 0 | 396 7 0 | 1186 7 0 |
| **109 in. Wheelbase Pick-up:** | | | |
| Basic Vehicle ... | 690 0 0 | | |
| De Luxe Vehicle ... | 710 0 0 | | |
| **Fire Engine** ... ... | 980 0 0 | | |

Land Rover cannot have helped.

So Rover embarked on designing its own diesel engine. Engine designer Jack Swaine drew up basic architecture that could also be used for a new four-cylinder petrol engine later on, but for the diesel his brief was to design an engine that had power and torque characteristics as close as possible to those of the existing petrol engine, so that the two engines could share the same gearbox and transmission components. In practice, the 2.0-litre diesel engine revved much more slowly than the existing 2.0-litre petrol type; it was also very noisy in a Land Rover which had very little trim to absorb that noise; and the diesel was physically larger than the petrol engine as well.

Rover coped with this need for extra space in the most cost-effective way possible. Instead of redesigning the engine bay, they moved the front axle and its springs two inches forwards to make room for the diesel engine. The redesigned chassis suited the existing petrol engine as well, and so the 86-inch Land Rover became an 88-inch type and the 107-inch model became a 109-inch. The exception was the 107-inch Station Wagon, which had only just gone into production; Rover were unwilling to spend more money on redesigning the front end of its special chassis, and so it kept its original wheelbase and could not be ordered with the new diesel engine.

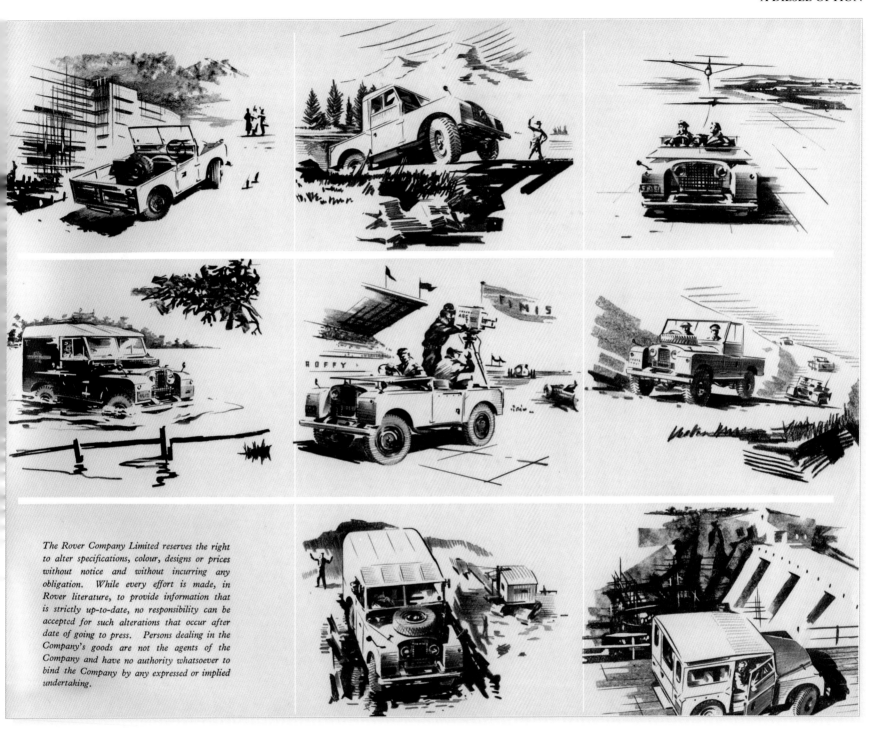

Rover spread the cost of the changes by introducing the new longer wheelbases in June 1956. To avoid questions about the reasons for the changes in dimensions, and to deflect even more difficult ones about why the 107-inch Station Wagon did not have a 109-inch wheelbase, they adopted a new policy of calling the 88-inch models "regular" Land Rovers and the 109-inch models "long" types.

The diesel engine then arrived in June 1957. Sales were quite slow in the beginning, not least because the engine quickly developed a reputation for cracking its cylinder head. Nevertheless, it gradually gained acceptance and would remain available until a larger-capacity version was introduced in 1961. The 88s and 109s remained in production only until April 1958. They have therefore always been relatively rare, whether as petrol or diesel models.

*The theme of versatility was continued with these drawings. They really do seem to be 88s, too, with a noticeably short section of wing ahead of the front wheelarch.*

*The new naming policy never really worked, even at Rover. This 1957-season catalogue used the 109-inch and "long" names in tandem. Standard Land Rover green was available for the long-wheelbase models by this time.*

# 109" WHEELBASE 'LONG' LAND-ROVER

Another version of the four-wheel drive Land-Rover is the 109 in. wheelbase 'Long' vehicle with all-purpose open body. The cab is fully enclosed and, if required, a weather-proof hood can be supplied at extra cost to protect the load space. As with its 88 in. wheelbase counterpart, the 109 in. is a model that has a great number of applications, its extra capacity making it a load carrier of exceptional merit.

For difficult cross-country work loads of 1,200 lb. (544 kg.) can be carried in addition to the driver and two passengers, while on journeys using more normal road surfaces, payloads of 1,500 lb. (680 kg.) can be satisfactorily dealt with.

Two types of the 109 in. wheelbase 'Long' Land-Rover are available : the standard model having a normally equipped cab, and the de luxe model with special interior upholstery and trim providing extra comfort for driver and passengers. A wide choice of other optional equipment is also available to ensure characteristic Land-Rover versatility.

*The diesel engine option crept into sales literature almost by stealth in June 1957. The cover of this catalogue showed business as usual with a Land Rover around the farm.*

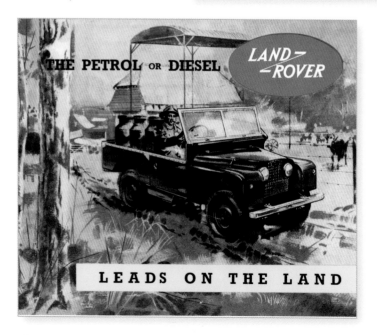

*The basic configuration of the Land Rover was unchanged, despite the extra two inches in the wheelbase.*

GEARBOX

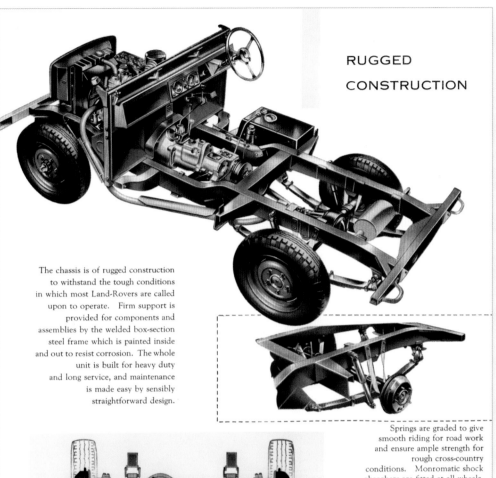

RUGGED

CONSTRUCTION

The chassis is of rugged construction to withstand the tough conditions in which most Land-Rovers are called upon to operate. Firm support is provided for components and assemblies by the welded box-section steel frame which is painted inside and out to resist corrosion. The whole unit is built for heavy duty and long service, and maintenance is made easy by sensibly straightforward design.

Springs are graded to give smooth riding for road work and ensure ample strength for rough cross-country conditions. Monromatic shock absorbers are fitted at all wheels.

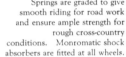

Front and rear axles of the 4-wheel drive Land-Rover are of spiral bevel design. They are exceptionally reliable and give long trouble-free service.

**ROVER DIESEL ENGINE . . .**

**. . . POWERFUL,**

**ROBUST,**

**ECONOMICAL**

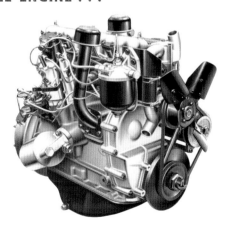

*The new engine was important enough to merit its own sales catalogue, separate from that for the vehicles. The cutaway drawing shows that it had overhead valves with a camshaft driven by roller chain, and that the fuel distribution pump was driven from the camshaft by gears. On the later petrol derivative – which was in fact designed at the same time – the fuel pump location was used for a distributor. It was a very neat solution to commonising designs. The diesel engine was always intended for Land Rovers (even though it was later tried experimentally in Rover cars), but the cover of the special engine brochure notes that it was a Rover diesel engine, and that it was "fitted in" Land Rovers. Even though Land Rovers were far outnumbering the cars from Solihull, the old car company still held its head high.*

51

# PINTAUX-TYPE INJECTION NOZZLES

Fuel injection nozzles are of the Pintaux type which incorporate two jets. The auxiliary jet sprays the fuel into the hottest portion of the combustion chamber and enables the engine to be started easily from cold. The main jet comes into operation at normal running speeds. Glow plugs are also fitted as an additional aid to starting the engine in extra low temperatures. They are controlled from the instrument panel and their use for a brief period before starting ensures an instantaneous result with the minimum of current consumption.

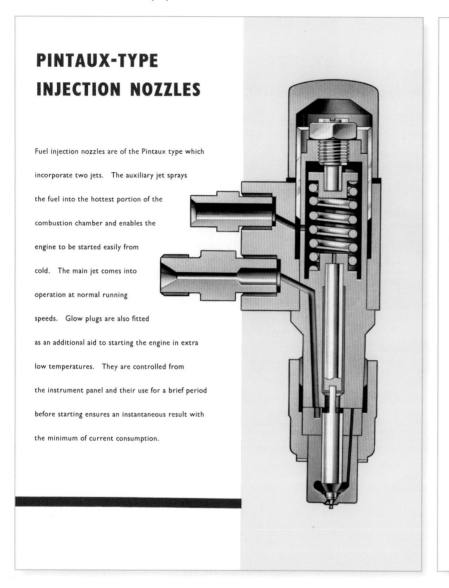

# RUGGED CYLINDER BLOCK

The cylinder block is an extremely rigid casting with an integral water distribution gallery which feeds the coolant round the cylinders through four jets. The cylinder block walls extend to below the crankshaft bearing split line to give added rigidity, while particular care has been taken in the arrangement of the cylinder head holding down bolts to ensure an efficient seal between block and head.

# WET CYLINDER LINERS

Wet cylinder liners are fitted in the Rover diesel engine. Their uniform and hard-wearing structure ensures very long life and they are accurately positioned in the cylinder block, being easily removed and replaced during overhaul.

# OVERHEAD VALVES

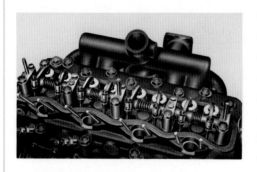

The overhead valves are operated by push rods and rockers from a chain-driven camshaft. Valve heads are of large diameter to give the most efficient breathing and they are cooled by ample water passages between the ports. Rubber rings are fitted to all valve guides to maintain good oil sealing.

# CYLINDER HEAD

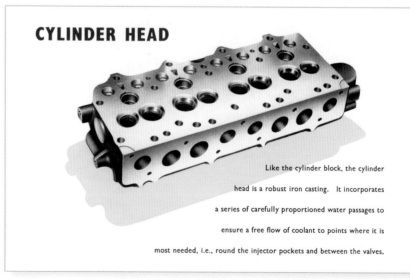

Like the cylinder block, the cylinder head is a robust iron casting. It incorporates a series of carefully proportioned water passages to ensure a free flow of coolant to points where it is most needed, i.e., round the injector pockets and between the valves.

# HYDRAULIC TIMING CHAIN TENSIONER

The camshaft is driven from the crankshaft by a Duplex roller chain on which tension is maintained by a hydraulic tensioner which is fed with oil from the engine lubricating system. It exerts pressure on the chain by means of a jockey sprocket, and ensures smooth and silent operation throughout the life of the engine. At engine idling speeds when oil pressure is low a special ratchet device keeps the tensioner in position and prevents the chain from slackening. A rubber damper pad is also fitted on the taut side of the chain to prevent whip.

# PISTONS AND CONNECTING RODS

Pistons are made of low expansion aluminium alloy and have provision for three compression rings and two oil control rings. The lower oil control ring is not initially required but can be fitted at a later stage in the life of the engine to counteract any increase in oil consumption after arduous and prolonged service. The familiar recess used in conjunction with the latest Ricardo Comet combustion chamber is cast into the piston crown. Connecting rods are of forged steel and incorporate a jet hole through which oil from the big-end bearings is squirted on to the thrust side of the cylinder walls. The upper part of the big-ends is so made that pistons and connecting rods may be withdrawn upward through the cylinder bores to facilitate servicing.

# CAMSHAFT WITH SPECIALLY DESIGNED CAMS

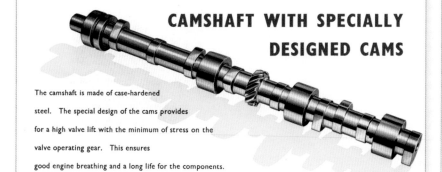

The camshaft is made of case-hardened steel. The special design of the cams provides for a high valve lift with the minimum of stress on the valve operating gear. This ensures good engine breathing and a long life for the components.

# COUNTERBALANCED CRANKSHAFT

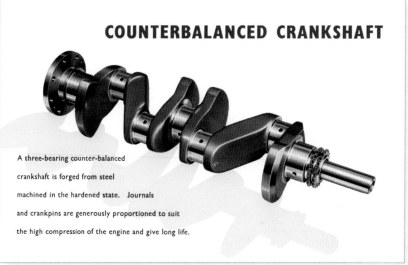

A three-bearing counter-balanced crankshaft is forged from steel machined in the hardened state. Journals and crankpins are generously proportioned to suit the high compression of the engine and give long life.

## RICARDO COMET V COMBUSTION CHAMBER

The Ricardo Comet V combustion chamber is of an exceptionally efficient design which ensures the highest possible degree of air utilisation. Fuel is sprayed into the hottest zone of the compressed air in the chamber when the engine is started from cold and is directed tangentially in the direction of air swirl for normal running. This is an important feature providing for the complete combustion of the fuel/air mixture and the most economical operation of the engine. A heat-resistant steel thimble is fitted into the injection nozzle cavity to give extra long life to the nozzle by preventing the hot gases from circulating round it.

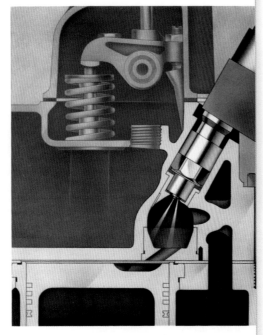

## CAV. DPA. INJECTION PUMP WITH MECHANICAL GOVERNOR

The CAV. DPA. injection pump may briefly be described as a single-cylinder, opposed plunger, inlet metering distributor pump. It incorporates an all-speed mechanical governor which operates during normal running, and in stationary work when the power take-off drives are in use. This type of injection pump has many advantages, being compact in construction, relatively simple in design and containing no ball or roller bearings, gears or highly stressed springs. The complete pump is an air-tight unit in which pressure is maintained thus preventing the entry of dust, water or other foreign matter during operation. No special lubrication arrangements are necessary since the pump lubricates itself with the filtered fuel that it handles.

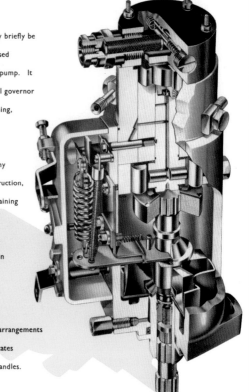

## COPPER-LEAD BEARINGS

Main and big-end bearing shells are of copper-lead with tin overlay. Bearings of this type are well-known for their great lasting qualities and are, in fact, used in all Rover engines.

*The special diesel engine brochure went into a great deal of detail about the features of the engine. Rover clearly thought it was important to do so, probably because diesel engines were unfamiliar to many potential customers. As for customers who did understand diesel engines, there was interest in how Rover had gone about downsizing, because most diesel engines in the 1950s were of 4.0 litres or more and were found in trucks and buses.*

## ROLLER-TYPE TAPPETS

One of the many interesting features of the Rover diesel engine is the novel design of the roller-type tappets. The roller which follows the cam runs in a lead tin-plated bronze shoe which in turn slides in a steel tappet guide. In this way the high valve lifts and consequent high accelerations needed for good engine breathing are obtained with the absolute minimum of wear on the cams. Here is another important contribution to the efficiency and long life of the engine.

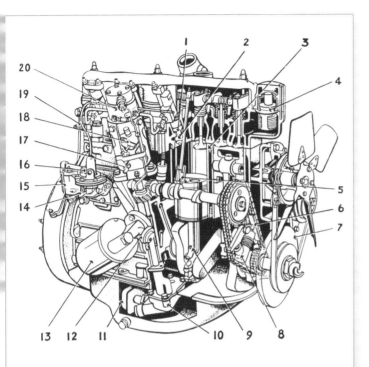

1. Pintaux Injection Nozzle.
2. Ricardo Comet V Combustion Chamber.
3. Wet Cylinder Liners.
4. By-pass Thermostat.
5. Roller Tappets.
6. Rubber Damper Pad.
7. Crankshaft Vibration Damper.
8. Hydraulic Timing Chain Tensioner.
9. Oil Jet to Cylinder Walls.
10. Oil Pump.
11. Gauze Strainer.
12. Oil Pressure Warning Light Switch.
13. Large Capacity Full-Flow Oil Filter.
14. Hand Priming Lever.
15. Sediment Bowl.
16. Fuel Lift Pump.
17. Stop Lever.
18. Accelerator Lever.
19. Glow Plugs.
20. CAV.DPA. Injection Pump with Mechanical Governor.

*Though we have no way of knowing whether this vehicle had a diesel or a petrol engine, it was a 109-inch model built between 1956 and 1958. This Land Rover was equipped as a mobile lubrication unit, and it was used for maintenance of heavy machinery in the field. The equipment itself was by Wakefield, who had recently been bought out by Castrol, and was one of the aftermarket conversions "approved" by the Special Projects Department.*

The major work of the Special Projects Department in approving conversions coincided with the start of the Series II era, and only the very first approved conversions were pictured on earlier vehicles. These are two of them. The Fuller tanker was more of a trailer than anything else, but depended on the Land Rover's PTO to drive its pump.

# C12 MOBILE RADIO SET

As approved by the Rover Co. Ltd. for use with the

*LAND-ROVER*

This high frequency communications equipment is equally suitable for fixed or mobile operation, and may easily be installed in any vehicle. Widely used by police and the British Army under arduous conditions, the C12 is fully approved by the Ministry of Supply.

Designed for a wide variety of fixed or mobile military applications, it is particularly suitable for police and special users in undeveloped areas where h.f. operation is permitted.

The C12 Mobile Radio Set can be used for speech or c.w. telegraphy, and is continuously tunable over the frequency range 1·6 – 10·0 Mc/s in two bands of 1·6 – 4·0 Mc/s and 4·0 – 10·0 Mc/s. Duplicate-tuned circuits with separate controls permit the pre-tuning of two frequency channels within these bands. A frequency selector is provided so that the operator may instantly switch to these channels. A frequency reconstituting circuit automatically nets the transmitter frequency to that of the receiver.

In daylight, under average conditions, the range between mobile stations is 30 miles for radiotelephony and 50 miles for c.w. The average ranges for fixed stations using 32-ft. whip aerials are 50 miles R/T and 75 miles c.w. With a horizontal end-fed aerial, point-to-point communication can be established over ranges of 500 miles or more, depending on propagation conditions.

A power supply unit can be supplied for use either on 12 or 24 volts. The set is sealed, is dust- and splash-proof, and will not be damaged by immersion in water for short periods. Suitable for use in any part of the world, the C12 Mobile Radio Set meets the standards of climatic durability laid down in the British Inter-Service Specification K114. Provision is made for crystal control which can be switched in as an alternative to the master oscillator.

# PYE TELECOMMUNICATIONS LIMITED
## NEWMARKET ROAD, CAMBRIDGE

# PUTTING ON THE STYLE

*All of a sudden, somebody at Solihull seemed to have realised that Land Rovers could be used for leisure pursuits as well as in farming and in light industry. The first catalogue for the Series II 88, issued in April 1958, showed the vehicle being used to tow a boat.*

*It was back to serious stuff for the 109 catalogue, though, and the truck cab model (as it was now called) was pictured at work in the oilfields of the Middle East. The cab has its own tropical roof, which was not fitted on models destined for temperate climates.*

General development on the Land Rover was a continuous process, and during the first half of the 1950s the company did not really think in terms of freshening the design cosmetically. The important thing was to improve it mechanically and structurally in line with demand.

However, two things occurred to change that. The first was that Austin determined to take a slice of the light 4x4 market, partly as a result of the work they had done in developing the Champ, which was a dedicated military vehicle that the British Army intended to use to replace their wartime Jeeps. The second was that Maurice Wilks had set up what was then called a Styling Department in 1953, handing over to David Bache the responsibility for the appearance of Rover products that had until then been his own.

The threat of competition from Austin was serious. Austin was a huge company by comparison with Rover, and if it threw its full weight behind a competitor for the Land Rover, Rover's future looked bleak. So it was important to improve the Land Rover to counter this threat. The new Austin, which became the Gipsy, was expected to reach the market in 1958, and so Rover began working towards an extensively improved Land Rover to be launched at the same time or slightly earlier. Subtle improvements could be made in many areas, such as widening the axles to improve stability, but one major improvement already under development was a new petrol engine, based on the same architecture as the Land Rover diesel engine.

By 1958, the Land Rover would have been in production for ten years, and its appearance had barely changed. So Rover decided that it needed a major facelift to help fight off the Austin competition. The job fell to David Bache. The exact sequence of events is still unclear, but it appears that Bache began by designing a new long-wheelbase Station Wagon – probably because the makeshift appearance of the vehicle Rover intended to release in 1956 made him wince. He came up with a remarkably elegant design, and Rover thought highly enough of the prototype vehicle to present it to the Royal Family. Slightly modified, it became the new Land Rover ten-seat Station Wagon, and the basic design became the basis for a completely re-styled Land Rover utility range as well.

There was no doubt that Bache's design was a huge improvement over what had gone before, and yet it remained practical as well as elegant. In fact, the design that characterised the Series II models introduced in April 1958 – exactly ten years since the Land Rover's announcement in Amsterdam – was so successful than it was still in use more than 50 years later, changed in only small details.

With the arrival of what Rover called the Series II Land Rovers, the older models built between 1948 and 1958 became known collectively as Series I types.

LAND-ROVER

The Long Land-Rover in standard open form is shown here. Hood sticks and hood, all-over body and cab hood, and detachable hard-top can be supplied at extra cost.

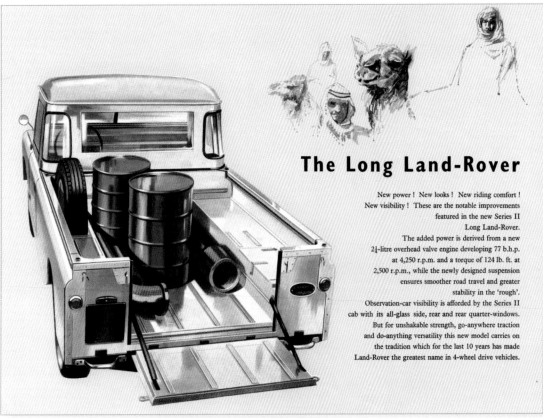

# The Long Land-Rover

New power ! New looks ! New riding comfort ! New visibility ! These are the notable improvements featured in the new Series II Long Land-Rover.
The added power is derived from a new 2¼-litre overhead valve engine developing 77 b.h.p. at 4,250 r.p.m. and a torque of 124 lb. ft. at 2,500 r.p.m., while the newly designed suspension ensures smoother road travel and greater stability in the 'rough'.
Observation-car visibility is afforded by the Series II cab with its all-glass side, rear and rear quarter-windows. But for unshakable strength, go-anywhere traction and do-anything versatility this new model carries on the tradition which for the last 10 years has made Land-Rover the greatest name in 4-wheel drive vehicles.

*The Series II 109 truck cab model was undeniably well-proportioned. The barrel-sides, turning out from the waist-line, not only covered the wide axle tracks but also gave the vehicle a simple feature line where before there had been none. Yet perhaps the crowning glory of the design lay in the new truck cab, with its curved quarter-windows. They were practical, giving good rearward vision, and added character as well.*

## The Land-Rover Regular Station Wagon

*The body is easily accessible from the rear of the vehicle*

Like all Land-Rovers the Long Station Wagon has four-wheel drive, and affords an ideal means of carrying personnel or equipment over difficult country. Its possibilities are numerous; airport, oilfield, survey and safari duties providing exceptional scope for its versatility and powers of progress.

As an alternative passenger or goods-carrying vehicle the seven-seater Land-Rover Regular Station Wagon has tremendous appeal in territories where tough and exacting conditions are likely to be met. As a personnel carrier it will accommodate three people in front and four on fold-away seats in the rear compartment. With the seats folded up, ample body space is available for the transport of goods and equipment of all kinds.

*The body style for the Series II 109 Station Wagon was a superb solution to the demands of the vehicle, although it had still not been possible to put both door handles at the same height! The 88 Station Wagon was simply a shorter version of the same thing, although the light-coloured one here seems to have been stretched and lowered a little by the artist's imagination. Customers were used to such licence in car advertising of the period.*

Based on a fully box-sectioned chassis of immense strength and having a completely rust- and corrosion-proof body of aluminium alloy, the Land-Rover will outlast any similar type of vehicle. A rugged machine that needs no coddling, it can be left out of doors year in, year out, in any weather, in any climate.

*Full length canvas hood*

*Three-quarter length hood*

*Three-quarter length hood with side windows for Export*

Land-Rovers have now completed ten years' uninterrupted operation on and off the roads of the world. During this time they have built up a record of unremitting service that can never be equalled. Their number-less activities in undeveloped territories have become legendary.

To-day, the new, sleeker Series II Land-Rover takes the field. Improved in riding comfort and all-round convenience in operating and servicing, it continues the tradition of versatility, unstoppability and toughness for which its predecessors are justly famed.

After 10 years, Land-Rover engineers know what they are up against and have built the new model accordingly. There can be no substitute for operational experience—there *is* no substitute for the 4-wheel drive Land-Rover.

## The Regular Land-Rover

The Regular Land-Rover is provided, as standard equipment, with a completely weather-proof canvas hood. A truck-type cab, giving all-round visibility, and a detachable hard-top (left) can also be fitted at extra cost. Hard-tops with side windows are available for export models.

*There were three different types of canvas tilt for the 109-inch models. The "full-length canvas hood" was more common overseas than in the UK, where buyers tended to prefer a metal cab. When that metal cab – "truck cab" – was fitted, the canvas tilt covered only the load bed. It was available with windows for export, so making the rear a nicer place to sit when the vehicle was carrying passengers. However, the possibility of carrying passengers in the back incurred extra tax in Britain, so the sides of the hood remained resolutely plain.*

*The basic open 88 was still available with soft top or hardtop, the latter being seen here with the tropical roof supplied only on models destined for hot countries.*

*Central to the improvements made for the Series II models was the new petrol engine. Based on the same OHV design as the diesel type, it had a larger capacity of 2¼ litres; this had been achieved by omitting the wet liners of the diesel version. When running properly the "Two-and-a-quarter" was a beautifully smooth engine, smooth enough to earn a place in Rover saloons as well between 1959 and 1962. The engine continued to power Land Rovers right through to 1981, when it was redesigned with five main bearings instead of three and renamed a 2.3-litre (though its dimensions remained the same) for another four years of life. Then upgraded to 2.5 litres, it survived in production until 1992, by which time the basic design was more than 35 years old.*

The 2¼-litre overhead valve petrol engine develops 77 b.h.p. at 4,250 r.p.m. and has a torque of 124 lb. ft. at 2,500 r.p.m. Thus, there is abundant power available for vehicle operation, hauling trailers or driving machinery. Power that is smooth and willing for normal work ; slogging, determined power for tough assignments. This is an outstandingly reliable engine, its robust construction giving it a long and trouble-free life.

**PETROL *Power* to go anywhere**

The 2-litre diesel engine of Rover design and construction gives further versatility to the Land-Rover by increasing its efficiency and economy in conditions favouring diesel operation. A truly rugged, four-cylinder unit, the Rover diesel engine develops 52 b.h.p. at 3,500 r.p.m. Its speed range is sufficiently close to that of the Land-Rover petrol engine that the same transmission units may be used for both.

*The 2.0-litre diesel engine remained available in the Series II. It had stopped cracking its cylinder heads and seemed slightly more refined than at its launch in 1957, but it was still noisy.*

**DIESEL *Power* for long range economy**

LAND-ROVER

the

world's

most

versatile

vehicle

The gearbox remained unchanged for Series II models, and still drove through a transfer box giving high ratios for road work and low ratios for off-road. The forest of levers was such a familiar sight that it made the front cover of the 1959 sales brochure. Ever since the free-wheel control had been eliminated in 1949, the lever with the yellow knob had engaged drive to the front axle and the one with the red knob had selected low ratios in the transfer box. Selecting low ratio automatically selected drive to all four wheels as well. The gear lever for the primary gearbox simply had a black knob.

## versatile transmission

This well-known, operationally-proved gearbox and transfer box unit is used in all Land-Rover models. The main gearbox has four forward speeds and one reverse with synchromesh on third and top. Additional ratios are provided by the transfer box so that in all, eight forward and two reverse speeds are available. Selected as necessary with the two- or four-wheel drive they give to the Land-Rover its remarkable go-anywhere qualities.

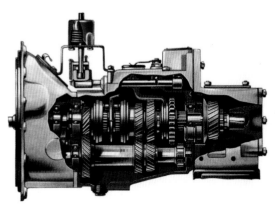

In addition to the normal gear control, a yellow-knobbed, push-down lever selects two- or four-wheel drive in the high ratio range. The lever with red top engages low ratio with four-wheel drive.

Quick-action catches are used to secure the tailboard on Series II Land-Rovers. They operate easily and cannot be inadvertently detached and lost.

*Not immediately obvious from the chassis picture, which shows a diesel Series II 88, is how the wider tracks had been accompanied by outrigged rear springs.*

# rugged chassis construction

Of great strength and rigid box-section construction, the Land-Rover chassis will stand up to any strain or stress occasioned by the vehicle's go-anywhere, do-anything duties. During the dipping process, paint flows throughout the inside of the frame as well as over its outside surface to give maximum resistance to corrosion. The whole unit is of straightforward design affording exceptional ease of maintenance. The diesel-engined Regular chassis is illustrated.

# tough suspension

Rear suspension has been redesigned for Series II vehicles, with the springs now mounted on sturdy outrigger brackets to give greater overall stability. The springs themselves are of lower rate and, operating in conjunction with new shock absorbers, provide a well balanced ride for driver, passengers and load.

*Though used to illustrate an early Series IIA catalogue, this is actually the 109-inch chassis of a Series II model*

# The Land-Rover Long Station Wagon

Based on the 109-inch wheelbase chassis the Long Station Wagon is a ten-seater, go-anywhere personnel carrier.

The seating arrangement provides accommodation for three people in front, three on the back seat and four, facing inward, on additional seats fitted to the rear wheel boxes. If the wheel box seats are folded up and the back seat is lowered right forward the whole body is available for load carrying.

Additional seats are included in the vast selection of optional extra equipment that is available for the Regular Land-Rover. Fitted to the wheelbox on each side of the body, they provide accommodation for four people.

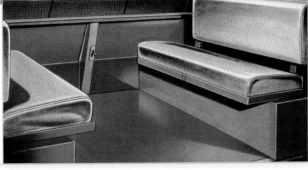

*The interior of the long-wheelbase Station Wagon had been re-drawn by this time, and featured the correct type of rear door window. Compare this with the 107 Station Wagon interior illustrated on page 46. The inward-facing bench seats were standard on long-wheelbase Station Wagons and could also be bought as an option for other models, but the 88 Station Wagons had four individual seats in the rear.*

*Despite other improvements, the driving compartment was much the same as before, and describing the cab as "completely weatherproof, dust and draught-free" as this brochure does was simply laughable. Needless to say, the cab illustrated is the De Luxe type, with additional floor coverings and door trims.*

# cab comfort

The standard cab provides completely weatherproof, dust and draught-free accommodation for three people. Deeper cushions on Series II vehicles give an added degree of riding comfort.
An alternative, de-luxe cab is available as an optional extra, trimmed door casings and carpets being offered as additional refinements.

When required, the windscreen can be folded forward on to the bonnet. A rubber pad is fitted to the top of the windscreen frame for this purpose.

# practical power take-off

Land-Rover versatility is greatly enhanced by the provision of power take-off facilities. The equipment can be supplied at extra cost and enables various kinds of towed and standing machinery to be driven. There are four main types of power take-off unit : Rear, with splined shaft or pulley drive ; centre, with pulley drive ; front-mounted winch.

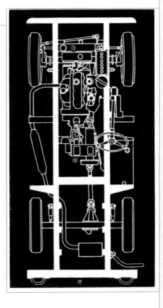

*Little details were going to matter in the battle against the Gypsy, and Land Rover made sure that potential buyers were aware of all of them.*

*The power take-offs and their attachments were the same as before, although their presentation in the catalogue was distinctly brighter. Rover really were trying hard to counter the threat from the Austin Gypsy.*

# The Land-Rover Long Fire Engine

Built on the Land-Rover four-wheel drive 109-inch wheelbase chassis, the Long Fire Engine provides greater load- and personnel-carrying capacity than the Regular model, while retaining all its essential go-anywhere features. The all-weather truck cab, fitted as standard on this model, gives generous accommodation for driver and two passengers, and a seat mounted in the rear of the vehicle, facing aft, will carry two additional persons. General fire fighting equipment is the same as that supplied with the Regular Fire Engine.

*The extra load capacity of the 109-inch chassis made it far better suited than the 88 to fire engine duties. For 1959, there were therefore fire engines from Solihull on both chassis, now the responsibility of a department set up in late 1957 to take over responsibility for all conversions of the basic vehicle. The new department was called Special Projects, and it ran a scheme which granted Land Rover Approval to after-market specialist conversions after inspecting them to make sure they did not compromise the integrity of the base vehicle. "Approved" conversions were also advertised through Land Rover showrooms, and farming out the work involved to specialists in this way took much of the heat off Special Projects themselves. By mid-1959, they had commissioned fire appliance specialists Carmichael's of Worcester to build Land Rover fire engines, and other specialists were added to the list later. So Solihull did not build many Series II fire engines like those illustrated here.*

*Truck cab, and the hose couplings and blanking caps illustrated are optional extras*

# The Land-Rover Regular Fire Engine

The Land-Rover Regular Fire Engine is a compact, extremely mobile, self-contained appliance that can deal quickly with outbreaks which are out of reach of larger vehicles. Narrow tracks, moorland, factories, farms or forests—no place is inaccessible to this Land-Rover. Standard equipment includes ; 40 gallon first aid water tank, 120 feet of rubber hose coiled on a drum, hose lockers and pump control panel. The pump itself has a rating of 210 gallons per minute at 100lb. per sq. in. pressure for a 10 foot lift.

**Forage harvesting**

THE 4-wheel drive Land-Rover is the farmers' all-the-year-round, do almost anything, go anywhere vehicle.

work in a muddy field, driven immediately to market or elsewhere at nearly 70 m.p.h. and retur

some entirely different task. And its light alloy bodywork ensures complete freedom from corrosion. Wha

has anything like this outstanding versatility and mobility?

Farmers in Britain and throughout the world are appreciating more and more the innumerable possibi

and are employing them in ever increasing numbers.

They all agree that there is no substitute for the

petrol or diesel Land-Rover. Some of the Land-Rover's

many uses on the farm are illustrated on this page.

**Loading churns**

**Circular saw**

**Rounding up the flock**

**Towing a seed drill**

**Gang mowing**

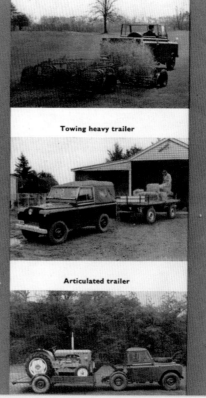

**Crop spraying**

**Pumping with tailboard-fitted unit**

**5-ton capacity winch**

**Towing heavy trailer**

**Mowing hay**

**Using a pneumatic pick**

**Swathe turning**

**Articulated trailer**

**Land levelling or snow clearance**

## ORRODIBLE BODYWORK

...e taken from

...ive machinery or take on

...farm vehicle

...f these amazing vehicles

**Trailer hauling**

**Pasture maintenance (topping)**

**Rotary brush cutter**

**Concrete mixing**

**Lubrication service**

**Manure spreading**

**Weed breaking**

**Handling liquid manure**

**Electric welder**

Yes, the Land Rover did still lead on the land, and this selection of thumbnail pictures showing Series IIs at work on the farm was designed to ram the point home. It was yet another illustration of the vehicle's versatility, but was there a deeper significance in the use of photographs rather than illustrators' artwork? During the 1960s, Land Rover would again use commercial artists for publicity material, so perhaps this brochure deliberately used photographs to make the point that this versatility was all real and not just the product of an illustrator's imagination.

Suddenly, the bright brochures used for the launch of the Series II were replaced by distinctly dowdy ones. The green one was for 1959 and the brown one for 1960. What had happened? The explanation is almost certainly that the immediate threat from the Austin Gipsy had receded. The vehicle just wasn't as good as Rover had feared it might be, and so Solihull could get away with spending less money on its sales brochures.

*This was one of those advertisements that said it all: the Land Rover was supposedly pictured in Australia, and was of course the only vehicle that could get to Starvation Creek Road. There was, as the copywriter put it, "no substitute". The ad dates from 1960.*

*There were different requirements in Australia, where the long-wheelbase Land Rover had already proved its value as a flat-bed farm truck. As no body of that type was available from Land Rover, the major regional dealers made arrangements to have them built by local specialists. This was the one offered in 1958 on the Series II by Grenville Motors in Sydney, New South Wales.*

AT LEFT: The Table-top Land-Rover, with sides dropped, offers an uninterrupted loading area of 36 square feet. Loading height is 37 inches.

AT RIGHT: View showing the Table-top with sides raised.

**1**

**2**

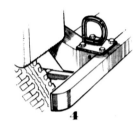
**3**

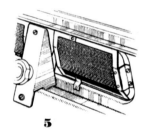
**4**

### 109" LONG WHEEL BASE SPECIFICATIONS

**ENGINE**—Four cylinders. Overhead inlet and exhaust valves; bore 3.562 ins.; stroke 3.5 ins.; capacity 139.5 cu. in.; maximum b.h.p. 77 at 4,250; maximum torque 124 lb. ft. at 2,500 r.p.m.; compression ratio 7 to 1.

**CLUTCH**—Single dry plate; 9 in. diameter.

**TRANSMISSION**—Transmission to rear and front axles by open propeller shaft via two-speed transfer box.

**GEARS**—Four forward speeds and reverse. Two-speed transfer box in conjunction with main gearbox gives 8 forward speeds and two reverse.

**BRAKES**—Hydraulically operated foot brakes requiring infrequent adjustment. Mechanically actuated hand brake operates on transmission shaft to rear axle.

**CHASSIS**—Welded steel box section of great strength. Protected against corrosion inside and outside, while conventional layout gives easy maintenance.

**SPRINGS**—Semi-elliptic front and rear—telescopic shock absorbers front and rear.

**TABLE-TOP VEHICLE PAYLOAD**
(Maximum)

3 persons plus 18 cwt. on good going. On rough work lighter loads are recommended.

### TABLE-TOP DIMENSIONS

| | | |
|---|---|---|
| (a) | Overall length of vehicle | 14' 9" |
| (b) | Enclosed tray length | 6' 2" |
| | Overall tray length | 6' 6" |
| (c) | Enclosed tray width | 5' 2" |
| | Overall tray width | 5' 6" |
| (d) | Height of sideboards | 1' 0" |
| (e) | Loading board. (Approx. height) | 2' 6" |
| (f) | Loading height | 3' 1" |

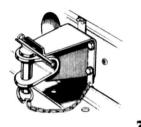
**5**

**6**

**7**

**8**

*As always, there was a huge variety of special equipment available for the Land Rover, and this illustration shows a selection of that available for the Series II models at the start of the 1960 model-year.*

**9**

**10**

**11**

**12**

A SELECTION OF ITEMS OF OPTIONAL EQUIPMENT: *1*, Locking door handles. *2*, Recirculating heater unit. *3*, Self-cancelling flasher switch and warning light. *4*, Lifting and towing ring. *5*, Fly screen for dash vent. *6*, Rubber pedal pads. *7*, Heavy duty towing pintle. *8*, Rear seat. *9*, Speedometer with trip recorder. *10*, Spare-wheel carrier (bonnet). *11*, Propeller shaft cover. *12*, Drawbar and extension for towing jaw

# MILITARY

**M**ilitary sales very soon began to account for a large proportion of the Land Rovers built every year. The Rover Company was more than pleased to list the overseas countries that had bought Land Rovers for their military forces, and in 1956 listed 17, in 1958 24 (though this was claimed to be a partial list), and in 1966 no fewer than 75. In more recent years, and especially since trouble first flared in the Middle East in the mid-1960s, they have been far more reticent, to protect political sensitivities.

Generally, Land Rovers were promoted to military buyers by

*The Special Air Service has always been a secretive regiment, not least in order to protect knowledge about its missions and methods. However, it was prepared to admit as early as 1957 that it was taking delivery of some specially-equipped Land Rovers – but not what they were for. There was a small batch of them, based on Series I 88-inch models.*

As the S.A.S. vehicles normally operate self-contained, storage space is provided for food, water and personal kit as well as ammunition.

*Land Rovers became the standard light 4x4 in the British Army in 1956. That was a tremendous honour, achieved in the face of direct opposition from the War Department's own specially-designed Austin Champ. It was also a huge help to sales, both to the British military and to others world-wide who looked to them for training and inspiration.*

direct personal contact or at military equipment shows. So there was no call for military sales brochures in the 1950s and 1960s. Nevertheless, there were some publications which were intended to be of use to Land Rover sales personnel, and some of those illustrated military derivatives. Most of the pictures in the section that follows came from a booklet produced during the 1960 season; the others are from catalogues published for the joint exhibitions staged by the Society for Motor Manufacturers and Traders and FVRDE at Chertsey.

*Only minor modification was needed to make the short-wheelbase Series I into a line-layer, suitable for laying communications cables.*

Truck, ¼-Ton, 4×4, C.L. (Land-Rover), S.A.S., 88″ Wheelbase. For Special Air Service duties, a modified Regular Land-Rover.

Truck, ¼-Ton, 4×4, C.L. (Land-Rover) Cargo, 88″ Wheelbase, fitted with line-laying equipment.

## FV 18047

## Truck Fire Fighting Airfield Crash Rescue
## (Rover 0·75 tonne 4 x 4)

**Description:** This vehicle has been developed to meet the requirement of MOD (RAF) for a vehicle for immediate rescue from crashed aircraft, to deal with aircraft wheel brake fires, and to act as a light auxiliary fire truck to escort aircraft at dispersals. The vehicle is based on the current commercial specification for the Landrover 109 in wheelbase Pick-up Truck. Changes have been made to the commercial specification to render the vehicle more suitable for Service use. These include such items as tyres with cross country tread, oil cooler and eight bladed fan, special towing attachment and strengthened rear cross member modified suspension FV pattern lights, brush guard to protect front of vehicle heavy duty front bumper, safety harness for crew members. The fire fighting equipment includes: two high-pressure dry-powder chemical extinguishers with discharge hoses and nozzles, ladder, saws—hand and compressed air operated, asbestos blankets and gloves, etc. The vehicle is also equipped with a high power searchlight and a site illuminating lamp.

FV Specification Number: Chassis 9255. Body 9255.

14

Another view of the line-laying vehicle.

A Land-Rover Crash Tender used by the Royal Naval Air Station at Gosport. It is fitted with full emergency equipment.

Truck, G.S. Cargo, 109″ Wheelbase, 4×4 (Land-Rover) Series 2, with hard-top cab.

Truck, G.S. Cargo, 109″ Wheelbase, 4×4 (Land-Rover) Series 2. The full-length canvas hood is fitted to this vehicle.

*Special derivatives were built for airfield use, their duties ranging from extinguishing wheel fires to providing rapid crew rescue from a crashed aircraft. The Royal Naval Air Service crash tender is actually based on an 80-inch model; the RAF tender is a much later vehicle from the early 1960s of a type known as the ACRT (Air Crash Rescue Tender) and specially built for the purpose.*

*Truck cab 109s were of course available, but the standard British military 109 had a full-length soft-top. It was described as a GS (General Service) type.*

*The British military took large quantities of a purpose-built ambulance body on the 109 chassis. Later versions were equipped to take four stretchers. The angled rear end allowed the vehicle to negotiate the ramps of landing craft.*

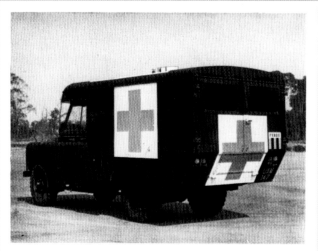

Ambulance 2-stretcher, G.S. 109″ Wheelbase, 4×4 (Land-Rover) Series 2. A special body to Service requirements fitted to the Land-Rover Long chassis.

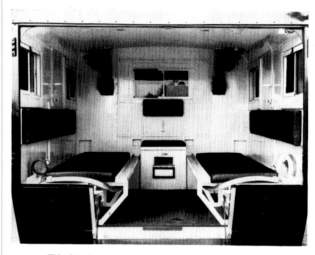

This view shows the general layout of the Ambulance interior.

Car, G.S. Utility Heavy, 109″ Wheelbase, 4×4 (Land-Rover) Series 2. A view into the Commander's Compartment.

*A much taller ambulance body had been developed in the mid-1950s for the RAF Mountain Rescue teams, and was built on the 107 chassis.*

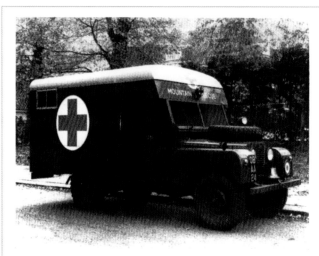

Truck, 4×4, C.L. (Land-Rover) Ambulance Special. Special body on Land-Rover Long chassis, for Royal Air Force Mountain Rescue.

Car, G.S. Utility Heavy, 109″ Wheelbase, 4×4 (Land-Rover) Series 2. This is the Land-Rover Long Station Wagon adapted to Service requirements.

*Even 109 Station Wagons had a role, though there were not many in British military service, and most were used as commander's vehicles.*

A fully loaded and equipped Land-Rover of the British Army goes aboard its transport aircraft.

Dropped by parachute, this Land-Rover in its special shock-resistant harness has landed safely and will be ready for action in a very few minutes.

EXHIBIT NO. **15**                    F.V. 18501

### Truck 1 ton Airportable General Purpose 4 x 4 (Scheme A) (with flotation kit)

**Description:** This vehicle is as Exhibit No. 14 but is shown fitted with flotation kit to enable the vehicle to cross inland water obstacles. The kit comprises four rubberised fabric air bags which are inflated by the vehicle exhaust system. Each bag is supported by a light alloy framework which can be quickly dismantled for stowage on the vehicle. Water propulsion is provided by a propeller mounted on the driving shaft to the rear axle, aided by rotation of the rear wheels.

Height: 7′ 0″ (*2·13 m.*).  Length: 21′ 10″ (*6·65 m.*).
  (over hood)
Width: 11′ 2″ (*3·40 m.*).  Wheelbase: 9′ 1″ (*2·77 m.*).
Track: Front 4′ 3½″ (*1·31 m.*).  Rear 4′ 3½″ (*1·31 m.*).
Weight: Unladen 4,255 lb. (*1,930 kg.*).  Laden 6,719 lb. (*3,048 kg.*).
**Note:** The data given below is for basic vehicle without flotation kit).

30

*Airportability was an important requirement, and Land Rovers were often dropped into the operating zone by parachute. In the early 1960s, a special long-wheelbase model was developed for the British Army; it could be stacked two-high in a transport aircraft and could also float across rivers when equipped with large buoyancy bags inflated from its exhaust. However, the development of heavy-lift helicopters meant that it was no longer needed.*

Land-Rovers of the Parachute Regiment on parade. The Commander's Car is fitted with seats inside the body.

A specially prepared Regular Land-Rover of the Royal Navy, used by H.M. The Queen on her visit to H.M.S. Eagle in April 1959.

*Short-wheelbase models were adapted for review purposes. They were generally simpler than the ones built specially for the Royal Family that were used for similar purposes.*

*The Indonesians were clearly not troubled by the idea of everyone knowing they used Land Rovers. The lower picture shows one equipped as a mobile anti-aircraft gun.*

Indonesian troops using a long wheelbase Land-Rover as a personnel carrier, a function it admirably fulfils.

Another Indonesian Army Land-Rover with a light anti-aircraft gun mounted in the body.

EXHIBIT NO. **24**

## Truck Cargo (Rover 1½ ton 4 x 4)

(Project State—Under Development)

**Description:** This vehicle was designed to meet a requirement for a G.S. 30 cwt load carrier. It has a diesel engine and all wheel drive. Front wheel drive selection is controlled by the driver and is available in all gear ratios. The vehicle shown is a prototype and is fitted with a manufacturer's body. In production G.S. type cargo or specialist bodies could be fitted. The load platform area is suitable for carrying the 1 ton container at Exhibit No. 47.

Height: 8′ 8½″ (*2·66 m.*).   Length: 15′ 6½″ (*4·73 m.*).
Width: 7′ 3¼″ (*2·215 m.*).   Wheelbase: 9′ 4″ (*2·84 m.*).
Track: Front 5′ 6″ (*1·675 m.*).   Rear: 5′ 6″ (*1·675 m.*).
Weight: Unladen 7,460 lb. (*3,390 kg.*).   Laden: 10,850 lb. (*4,290 kg.*).

50

*The back body of a short-wheel-base Land Rover was a good place to mount a weapon. The Spanish Army were pioneers in fitting the US-made 106mm recoilless rifle to turn their Land Rovers into tank destroyers.*

Spanish troops manning a 106 mm. recoiless gun mounted in the body of an 88″ wheelbase Land-Rover.

*Military sales of the Land Rover were so important to Rover that the company would bend over backwards to meet special requirements – especially if they were British. In the first half of the 1960s, the War Department thought it needed a 30cwt forward control truck, but was not impressed with the standard Land Rover Forward Control. So Land Rover built one to order; the first prototype was on a 120-inch wheelbase but was considered too big, so a second one was built on a 112-inch wheelbase. The War Department then changed its mind; the project was cancelled and the 112-inch prototype became the Rover works breakdown truck. Painted bright yellow and always known as Buttercup, it still survives today.*

# THEY ALSO SERVED

Those companies that supplied components for the Land Rover rarely advertised the fact, although they did swarm to get their names in lights when British Engineering & Transport magazine ran a special Land Rover supplement in November 1959. The Series II was by then more than 18 months old, so it was hardly "new", as some of the ads seemed to suggest.

*Of course, Land Rover made sure they had their own advertisement in a prominent position, and this was it. The 88-inch soft top model is a very early one and may be one of the very first, because this picture was issued to the press at the launch of the Series II in April 1958.*

*Galvanising was not one of the processes carried out at the Rover factory, but was sub-contracted to at least two Midlands companies. Both of them – Arkinstall Brothers Ltd in Birmingham and Midland Galvanizers Ltd – made sure they featured among the advertisers in that November 1959 publication.*

77

In the LAND ROVER you'll see **VYBAK** REGD.

FLEXIBLE CLEAR SHEET

The Land Rover has a rear window of VYBAK Flexible Clear Sheet because it combines toughness with clearer vision and greater flexibility.
This means that the rear flap can be rolled without cracking the window. VYBAK Flexible Clear Sheet is non-inflammable, shatter-proof and durable. It resists crazing, warping and discoloration.
VYBAK Rigid, Semi-rigid or Flexible Clear Sheet, is used for the side-screens or rear windows of every British sports car.

*Please write for samples and further details.*

# BAKELITE LIMITED

REGD.

*Bakelite Limited manufacture an extensive range of plastics materials and maintain a technical service unequalled in the industry. No matter what your plastics problems, this service is at your disposal. SLOane 0898 is the telephone number.*

12-18 GROSVENOR GARDENS · LONDON SW1 · SLOane 0898
TGA VS28

*The "plastic" windows in soft tops were made of Vybak, a product of the Bakelite company better known for the hard plastic that carried their name in the 1940s and early 1950s.*

*Berger Paints was one of the leading UK suppliers of motor vehicle finishes, and had been supplying Rover for many years.*

It's **Berger** for the Land-Rover!

**The toughest, finest finishes for all types of vehicle**

**TOUGH THROUGH AND THROUGH:** That's the Land-Rover. Right from its rugged engine to its long-lasting Berger finishes.
The Rover Company has used Berger paints for the Land-Rover since the vehicle was first introduced in 1948. And they use Berger paints for Rover private cars too.

Like other British motor manufacturers, who have used Berger vehicle finishes for over thirty years, they find them best for the job. Berger – the leading name in vehicle finishes.

**Visit our stand at the Motor Show No. 262 Avenue B, First Floor.**

**Berger Paints**
*Quality famous since 1760*

LEWIS BERGER (GREAT BRITAIN) LTD., Berger House, Berkeley Square, London, W.1 Telephone: Mayfair 9171

*BRITISH ENGINEERING & TRANSPORT (Land-Rover Supplement), November 1959* 25

**Ten-year testimonial**

For ten years the Birmabright bodywork of the Series I Land-Rover justified the designer's confidence in it. Now the Series 1 of this remarkable vehicle has been superseded by the Series II, but the bodywork material remains the same—tough, resilient, rustless Birmabright.

**Birmabright**
*Registered Trade Mark*
*Corrosion-resisting aluminium alloy*

BIRMABRIGHT LIMITED · WOODGATE WORKS · BIRMINGHAM 32
BH 223

*BRITISH ENGINEERING & TRANSPORT (Land-Rover Supplement), November 1959* 11

*The body structure of the Land Rover had always been made of Birmabright aluminium alloy, and here the material's manufacturers gained a share of the limelight.*

*Although the standard Land Rover differential of the time is often called a "Rover" differential because it was designed by Rover, in practice it was made by specialists Salisbury Transmission Ltd. That company later supplied heavy-duty components for Land Rovers, and those are known as "Salisbury axles".*

*CAV were the makers of the fuel distribution pump used on the Land Rover diesel engine. The company's name came from the initials of its founder, Charles Anthony Vandervell. It was bought by Lucas in 1926 and began developing fuel injection pumps in partnership with Robert Bosch Ltd in 1931, but Lucas then bought out the Bosch interests in 1937.*

*Long-wheelbase Land Rovers were proving their worth as light breakdown trucks, or "recovery vehicles" as the trade usually called them. Mann Egerton had taken the wise precaution of getting their conversions approved by the Special Projects Department.*

*Sparto were not the only supplier of lighting equipment for the Land Rover, but they were a major one during the Series II period.*

*First to get their fire appliance conversions approved by Land Rover were Carmichael & Sons of Worcester. From 1959, they were marketed under the name of Redwing, and replaced the Rover-built appliances. There were none on the 88-inch chassis at this stage, although demand soon persuaded Carmichael's to develop a design.*

*Borg & Beck were probably the best-known maker of clutches in Britain in the 1950s and 1960s, and were responsible for the standard clutch fitted to Series II Land Rovers. Sadly, their 1959 advertisement managed to show a Series I model rather than the latest Series II type …*

*Some of the specialist equipment on the Rover-built Land Rover fire appliances was supplied by George Angus & Co Ltd. This company merged with Hampshire Coach Bodies in 1963 to form HCB-Angus, which became a major supplier of Land Rover fire appliances for many years. The main picture shows Angus equipment on the Rover works fire engine, an 86-inch model dating from 1955, but the smaller picture shows a contemporary Series II 88-inch type.*

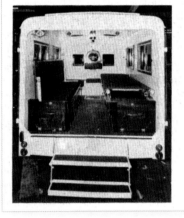
*Pilchers of Merton developed a coachbuilt aluminium ambulance conversion for the Series II 109-inch Land Rover. It was expensive, but a high-quality product. The company was among the first to get its conversions approved by the Special Projects Department.*

# THE 1960S

From mid-1961, Rover introduced a number of running changes to the Series II models, and from that point onwards Land Rovers became Series IIA types. The change of name suggested rather a lot more differences from the Series IIs than was really the case. There was indeed a big change for the diesel models, which now had an enlarged diesel engine with the same 2¼-litre capacity as the petrol engine. Otherwise, perhaps the biggest modification associated with the changeover to Series IIA production was that the battery was now under the seatbox rather than in the engine compartment.

The name Series IIA really came about by coincidence as much as anything else. At the time the new diesel engine was introduced, Rover changed to a new chassis numbering

*The 2¼-litre diesel engine had exactly the same architecture as the 2-litre type used in earlier and Rovers, but had the larger bore of the petrol engine and no cylinder liners. Though still quite raucous, it was rather more refined than the earlier engine. Rover advertised its arrival in some special sales catalogues, but it was the engine that mattered – the model change to Series IIA didn't get a mention. On the brochure at top right, the artist has taken special care to highlight the circular grille badge that read "Rover diesel". The badge was supposed to accompany the diesel engine on all Series IIAs so equipped, but was made of plastic and degraded quickly, so many owners simply removed it.*

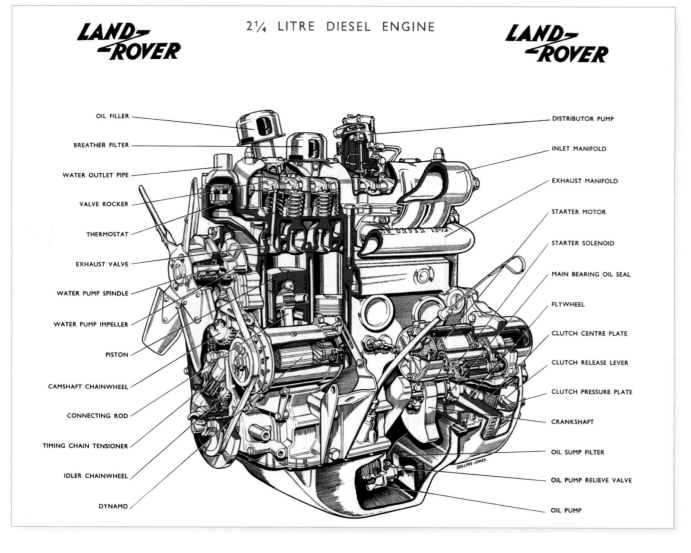

system for both cars and Land Rovers, adding a letter suffix to the numerical element to indicate changes that affected the servicing of the vehicle. The first Land Rover change of that kind was to the new diesel engine, so the 1962 models introduced in autumn 1961 became Series II, Suffix A or Series IIA types for short.

However, that new name stuck. When the suffix letter changed to a B in 1963, everybody continued to call the new models Series IIAs, because there were no major visible differences. And so it went on. By the time the final models were built in 1971 with a suffix H in their numbers, they were still known as Series IIA types.

There were some far-reaching changes elsewhere in the 1960s, however. Rover merged with British Leyland at the end of 1966, and with them of course went the Land Rover. For the rest of the Series IIAs' production period, however, BL was far too busy grappling with problems elsewhere in its vast empire to worry about micro-managing the Land Rover, and Solihull was left to carry on much as it always had.

*Visually, the Series IIA could only be distinguished from the Series II by a very close look; this would reveal that the bulkhead vents were now spot-welded rather than bolted to their hinges. As if to emphasise that point, 2861 UE on the cover of the brown brochure, issued for the 1962 season and touting the 2¼-litre diesel engine, was actually a 1961-model Series II.*

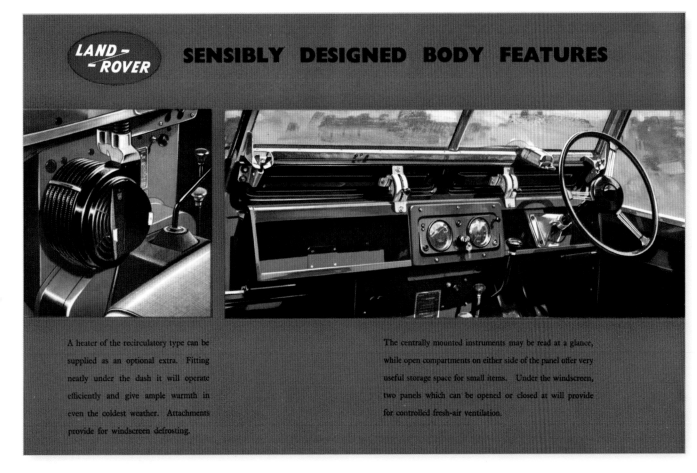

A heater of the recirculatory type can be supplied as an optional extra. Fitting neatly under the dash it will operate efficiently and give ample warmth in even the coldest weather. Attachments provide for windscreen defrosting.

The centrally mounted instruments may be read at a glance, while open compartments on either side of the panel offer very useful storage space for small items. Under the windscreen, two panels which can be opened or closed at will provide for controlled fresh-air ventilation.

*The Land Rover's "sensibly designed body features" had also not changed since the days of the Series II, and in fact the dashboard would not change until 1971. The heater, though, was replaced by a flat type towards the end of the 1960s.*

83

At the start of the 1960s, Rover undertook what today would have been called a branding exercise, and circulated their dealers with details of several items they could buy to enhance their showrooms. Some of these had been available earlier than 1961, of course, when the promotional booklet was circulated. The dealership could be made more visible from a distance by means of the flags or hanging signs shown here.

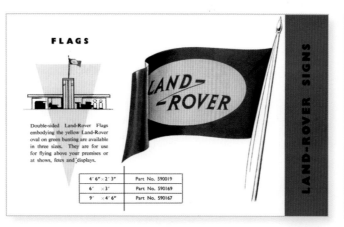

## FLAGS

Double-sided Land-Rover Flags embodying the yellow Land-Rover oval on green bunting are available in three sizes. They are for use for flying above your premises or at shows, fetes and displays.

| 4' 6" × 2' 3" | Part No. 590019 |
| 6'   × 3' | Part No. 590169 |
| 9'   × 4' 6" | Part No. 590167 |

LAND-ROVER SIGNS

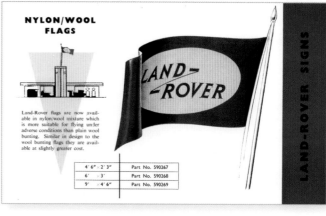

## NYLON/WOOL FLAGS

Land-Rover flags are now available in nylon/wool mixture which is more suitable for flying under adverse conditions than plain wool bunting. Similar in design to the wool bunting flags they are available at slightly greater cost.

| 4' 6" × 2' 3" | Part No. 590267 |
| 6'   × 3' | Part No. 590268 |
| 9'   × 4' 6" | Part No. 590269 |

LAND-ROVER SIGNS

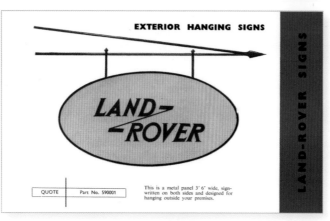

## EXTERIOR HANGING SIGNS

| QUOTE | Part No. 590001 |

This is a metal panel 3' 6" wide, signwritten on both sides and designed for hanging outside your premises.

LAND-ROVER SIGNS

## ROVER AND LAND-ROVER UNIVERSAL ILLUMINATED SIGNS
### FOR EXTERIOR AND INTERIOR USE

Carcase robustly constructed in aluminium. Bold panels in correct full colours measuring 22" × 34½". Illumination by four 2ft. long, 20 watt fluorescent tubes. Suitable for hanging, flush mounting, projecting, or can stand on wall. Completely weatherproof and easy to keep clean.

| ROVER/ROVER DOUBLE-SIDED SIGN | 590245 |
| ROVER SINGLE-SIDED SIGN | 590246 |
| LAND-ROVER/LAND-ROVER DOUBLE-SIDED SIGN | 590247 |
| LAND-ROVER SINGLE-SIDED SIGN | 590248 |
| ROVER/LAND-ROVER DOUBLE-SIDED SIGN | 590249 |

SUPPLEMENT

---

The next stage in reminding customers where they were was a branded rubber floor mat carefully positioned in the doorway.

There were signs for inside the showroom, too.

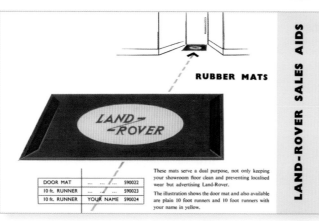

## RUBBER MATS

| DOOR MAT | ... | ... | ... | 590022 |
| 10 ft. RUNNER | ... | ... | ... | 590023 |
| 10 ft. RUNNER | YOUR NAME | 590024 |

These mats serve a dual purpose, not only keeping your showroom floor clean and preventing localised wear but advertising Land-Rover.

The illustration shows the door mat and also available are plain 10 foot runners and 10 foot runners with your name in yellow.

LAND-ROVER SALES AIDS

## INTERIOR NEON SIGNS

THESE SIGNS MUST BE COLLECTED BY YOU

| 250 v. A/C | BLACK | 590004 |
| | CLEAR | 590005 |

Measuring 30" × 15" this sign carries green neon tubing on a signwritten black or transparent back, the whole being contained in a perspex box and supplied complete with transformer.

LAND-ROVER SIGNS

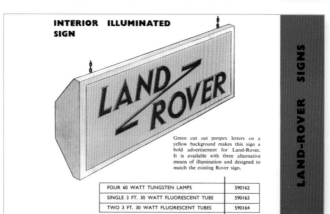

## INTERIOR ILLUMINATED SIGN

Green cut out perspex letters on a yellow background makes this sign a bold advertisement for Land-Rover. It is available with three alternative means of illumination and designed to match the existing Rover sign.

| FOUR 60 WATT TUNGSTEN LAMPS | 590162 |
| SINGLE 3 FT. 30 WATT FLUORESCENT TUBE | 590163 |
| TWO 3 FT. 30 WATT FLUORESCENT TUBES | 590164 |

LAND-ROVER SIGNS

## SHELF OR COUNTER SIGNS

| SALES & SERVICE | QUOTE Part No. 590042 |
| GENUINE PARTS | QUOTE Part No. 590007 |

For the spare parts counter or for hanging to advertise your service, these white signs have green cut-out perspex letters illuminated by four bulbs. Captioned "Sales and Service" or "Genuine Parts". Either of these will make an attractive display in your premises.

LAND-ROVER SIGNS

# TWELVE SEATER

**FOUR-WHEEL DRIVE · POWERFUL PETROL OR DIESEL ENGINE · FIVE DOORS · AMPLE SPACE**

# TWELVE SEATER

Based on the 109 in. Long chassis, the 12-seater Land-Rover is an immensely strong and powerful go-anywhere vehicle that completely solves the problem of transporting personnel to normally inaccessible places. Sporting parties and working parties will find it the toughest and most willing member of the team.

*Six-passenger accommodation at the back, accessible through the rear door or side doors.*

## 12-SEATER LAND-ROVER

The four-wheel drive Twelve-Seater Land-Rover is an immensely strong and powerful go-anywhere vehicle that completely solves the problem of transporting personnel to normally inaccessible places. It has seating for three people in front, three on individual tip-up seats behind, and six on inward-facing seats at the rear. Easy access to all the passenger accommodation is afforded by five doors, two on either side of the vehicle and one at the back.

As a personnel carrier, the Twelve-Seater Land-Rover is not subject to United Kingdom Purchase Tax and represents outstanding value for money.

# TWELVE SEATER

*The threat of new taxation prompted Rover to alter the specification of the long-wheelbase Station Wagons sold in Britain from 1962. Under new regulations, a 10-seater vehicle was a car and was subject to Purchase Tax, but a 12-seater was a commercial vehicle and therefore exempt. So while the 10-seater models remained in production for overseas markets, the British standard became a 12-seater. The new sales brochure was slightly misleading: in practice, the Station Wagon badge that hung below the Land Rover oval was not used on 12-seaters. The model was correctly illustrated in later catalogues. Inside there were now three individual seats in the middle, and longer inward-facing benches in the rear were supposedly capable of seating three passengers each. On the brochure picture, the faint trace of lines (not visible on the real thing) hinted at three separate positions. The reality, however, was that the there was still barely enough room for four normal-sized people in the back; if there were six in there, they had to be very small or very friendly.*

*Wide-opening doors at the side of the vehicle give excellent access to the interior.*

*Tip-up seats allow passengers to reach the rear compartment through the side doors when desired.*

THE 12-SEATER LAND-ROVER IS NOT SUBJECT TO U.K. PURCHASE TAX

*For the 1964 season, Rover once again focussed on the driver for the cover of the Land Rover sales brochure. The angle cleverly suggested that the viewer was in the driving seat. Standard models wouldn't have had those black floor coverings, though; those were part of the De Luxe trim specification.*

the world's most versatile vehicle

# POLICE AND MILITARY LAND-ROVERS

The Land-Rover is the ideal military light vehicle. Although originally designed for civilian use, its military potentialities were quickly recognised and today, Land-Rovers are in operation with the Police and Armed Forces of over fifty countries and territories around the world. It is standard equipment throughout the British Army.

A fleet of fifty Land-Rovers delivered to the Malayan Police for operations in the difficult areas of that country. This is a small part of a large Land-Rover force in use in Malaya.

Based on the Land-Rover Long Station Wagon but embodying many special features, this well-turned-out vehicle is in service with the Swiss Police.

Operations in the Aden Protectorate. The British Army Land-Rover might well be saying to the scout car, "Anywhere you can go, I can go too."

*Since the very earliest days, the Land Rover's value to police and military authorities had been accounting for a substantial number of sales. These 1964 images show the vehicles in use around the world; many of the vehicles pictured are in fact Series I types, so perhaps Series IIA deliveries were still subject to the sensitivity that affects information about deliveries to government authorities today*

A Bloodhound ground-to-air guided missile cradled on its special trailer. In flight it is powered by two ramjet engines; on the ground Land-Rover is the motive unit.

British paratroops taking their vehicle through troublesome terrain during manœuvres. Even Land-Rovers need a little help over some obstacles.

A desert convoy halts for a brief rest. The heat and sand of the arid Aden Protectorate are hard on men and machines but both are toughly built to withstand these conditions.

**1**

On its way to overseas duties, a Land-Rover loaded with equipment goes aboard its transport plane. With hood and hood-sticks stowed it is extremely compact to carry in this way.

**2**

A radio-equipped Land-Rover on patrol in rugged, inaccessible country. These vehicles frequently operate as individual units in conditions where complete reliability is essential for the safety of the crew.

**3**

Encased in its protective harness and with para-chutes billowing in the breeze, a Land-Rover arrives safely on the ground after being dropped from a transport aircraft.

**4**

Land-Rovers of the Para-chute Regiment on parade. The inspecting officer's vehicle is fitted with seats in the rear of the body, one of the many standard optional extras that are available.

## LAND ROVER – SERIES I, II, IIA & III

*The big news for 1967 was an optional six-cylinder engine in the 109-inch chassis. The engine itself was not new, having been designed in the late 1950s for Rover saloons. Detuned for Land Rovers so that it could run on poor-quality fuel, it had already appeared in the Forward Control models and, in car-style high-compression form, a special 109 Station Wagon sold only in North America. Though it was a smooth and refined engine, its fuel consumption could be alarming if it was used hard. It also did not take to use in a working Land Rover, although it rarely gave trouble in Station Wagons. The problem was that a working Land Rover spends much of its time slogging at or near maximum torque, and the car engine had not been designed to do that.*

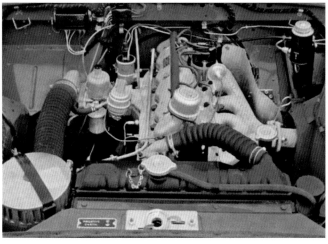

**SIX-CYLINDER PETROL ENGINE**
A six-cylinder, 2·6-litre petrol engine is now available as an additional alternative to the two four-cylinder units. It has been provided to give increased power output for those users whose operations call for above average road work.

*As the 1960s entered their second half, the carefully coloured drawings that had so often enhanced earlier Land Rover sales material gradually began to disappear in favour of colour photography. Nevertheless, drawings could still illustrate some things more effectively, and an artist's services were called on to produce these illustrations of the 88-inch and 109-inch chassis.*

The photographer assigned to producing a cover picture for the 1967 88-inch brochure nevertheless probably thought fondly of the good old days when he tried to get a decent farmyard shot. Or perhaps he should have remembered that you should never work with children or animals; as the unused shot from the sequence shows, cows never do what they are told.

Yet nobody could argue that colour photography lacked advantages; these images from catalogues issued in 1967 tell their story quite vividly.

For 1967, the Station Wagons were given their own sales catalogue. This reflected the special market that was developing for them; though shown on the cover as working vehicles, they were also beginning to attract a different type of buyer from the workhorse models. The illustrations of the 88's rear quarters were also captioned to stress comfort as much as practicality – although anybody who has spent much time in the back of an 88 Station Wagon will have some definite views on the level of comfort available.

Three front seats are also provided in the 7-seat Station Wagon. Trimmed and padded door casings and a trimmed roof lining are fitted, as in Long models. At the rear are four inward facing seats. In the down position (above, right) they offer comfortable travelling accommodation for personnel in an interior that is light and well-ventilated. They can be folded up (above, left) when not required for passengers so that the whole floor area can be used for the carriage of goods and equipment. Access to the rear compartment is gained through a side-opening door at the rear of the vehicle. A folding mounting step is provided.

109″ wheelbase 10-seater.

88″ wheelbase 7-seater.

109″ wheelbase 12-seater.

Land-Rover 4-wheel drive 7-seat, 10-seat and 12-seat Station Wagons have gained distinction throughout the world on major construction sites, on pioneering expeditions and safaris, at airports, with national and international organisations—anywhere, in fact, where unrestricted transport of personnel and equipment is needed all the year round in all climates and all conditions. Although outwardly similar to previous models, Station Wagons of today incorporate many mechanical refinements which have been evolved through years of operational experience.

## DIMENSIONS

### 7-SEATER STATION WAGON

| | | Ins. | Metres |
|---|---|---|---|
| A A | Wheelbase .. .. .. | 88 | 2·23 |
| BB | Track .. .. .. | 51·5 | 1·31 |
| CC | Overall length .. .. | 142·5 | 3·62 |
| DD | Overall width (over hinges) | 66 | 1·68 |
| EE | Overall height .. .. | 77·5 | 1·97 |
| A | Front cushion to accelerator pedal .. .. .. | 17·25 | ·438 |
| B | Front squab to steering wheel .. .. .. | 14·5 | ·368 |
| C | Headroom, front seat .. | 39 | ·99 |
| D | Front to rear of front cushion .. .. .. | 16·5 | ·42 |
| E | Width of front cushion .. | 18 | ·457 |
| F | Width of front centre cushion .. .. .. | 15 | ·381 |
| G | Width between front seats | 1 | ·025 |
| H | Top of front cushion to floor | 14·5 | ·368 |
| I | Front squab height .. | 18 | ·457 |
| J | Headroom, rear seat .. | 35 | ·890 |
| K | Top of rear cushion to floor | 14·5 | ·368 |
| L | Rear squab height .. | 18 | ·457 |
| M | Front to rear of rear cushion | 18 | ·457 |
| N | Width of rear cushion .. | 16 | ·406 |
| O | Width between front squab and rear cushion .. .. | 5 | ·127 |
| P | Width between rear cushions .. .. .. | 3 | ·076 |
| Q | Width across body between rear cushions (seats down) | 14 | ·357 |
| R | Width across body between rear cushions (seats up) .. | 38 | ·965 |
| S | Interior width of body at rear seats | 56·25 | 1·429 |
| T | Interior width of body between rear seat boxes | 36·3 | ·922 |
| U | Interior length of body between front squabs and rear door .. .. .. | 43 | 1·09 |

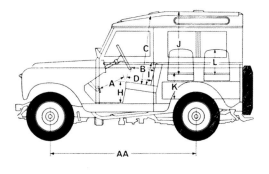

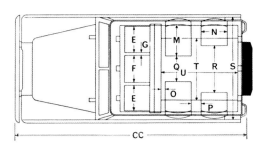

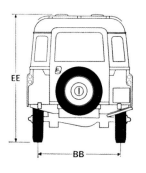

*Giving detailed interior dimensions was something that Rover did only for cars before 1967, although they had shown the dimensions of the long-wheelbase load-bed in some sales material. These dimensional drawings heralded a new attitude to the Station Wagons – although the market for them was nothing like it would become in the 1980s and later. Perhaps there was an element of preparing the buying public for the forthcoming Range Rover, which would be announced in 1970.*

## DIMENSIONS

### 10- AND 12-SEATER STATION WAGONS

| | | Ins. | Metres |
|---|---|---|---|
| A A | Wheelbase .. .. .. | 109 | 2·768 |
| BB | Track .. .. .. | 51·5 | 1·308 |
| CC | Overall length .. .. | 175·00 | 4·441 |
| DD | Overall width (over hinges) | 66·00 | 1·676 |
| EE | Overall height .. .. | 81·00 | 2·06 |
| A | Front cushion to accelerator pedal .. .. | 17·25 | ·438 |
| B | Front squab to steering wheel .. .. .. | 14·5 | ·368 |
| C | Headroom, front seat .. | 39·00 | ·991 |
| D | Front to rear of front cushion .. .. | 16·00 | ·406 |
| E | Width of front cushion .. | 18·00 | ·457 |
| F | Width of front centre cushion .. .. | 15·00 | ·381 |
| G | Width between front seats | 1·00 | ·025 |
| H | Top of front cushion to floor .. | 14·5 | ·368 |
| I | Front squab height .. | 17·00 | ·431 |
| J | Front squab to centre cushion .. .. | 12·5 | ·318 |
| K | Top of centre cushion to floor .. .. | 14·5 | ·368 |
| L | Centre cushion to front seat box .. .. | 18·75 | ·476 |
| M | Headroom, centre seat .. | 37·5 | ·952 |
| N | Front to rear of centre cushion .. .. | 14·5 | ·368 |
| O | Centre squab height .. | 15·00 | ·381 |
| P | Centre cushion width .. | 15·50 | ·393 |
| Q | Width between centre cushions .. .. | 1·00 | ·025 |
| R | Rear squab height .. | 12·5 | ·317 |
| S | Front to rear of rear cushion | 13·00 | ·330 |
| T | Top of rear cushion to floor | 12·25 | ·311 |
| U | Length of rear cushion (minimum) .. .. | 48·00 | 1·219 |
| V | Headroom, rear seat .. | 34·5 | ·876 |
| W | Width between rear seats | 28·75 | ·730 |
| X | Length of body between front squabs and rear door | 80·00 | 2·032 |
| Y | Interior width of body .. | 56·875 | 1·44 |
| Z | Front squab to centre cushion (10 str.) .. | 16·00 | ·406 |
| Z1 | Centre cushion width (10 str.) .. .. | 50·5 | 1·283 |
| Z2 | Front to rear centre cushion (10 str.) .. | 14·5 | ·368 |
| Z3 | Length of rear cushion (10 str.) .. | 32·25 | ·819 |
| Z4 | Front to rear of rear cushion (10 str.) .. .. | 13·00 | ·330 |

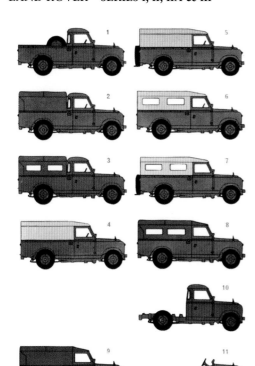

The basic model of the Long Land-Rover incorporates a truck cab and open body. All other body styles, as indicated here, are optional extras.

1. Basic model with truck cab and open body.
2. Three-quarter length canvas hood.
3. Three-quarter length canvas hood with side windows for export.
4. Hardtop with tailboard and top-hinged flap.
5. Hardtop with side-opening rear door.

6. Hardtop with tailboard, top-hinged flap and side windows for export.
7. Hardtop with side-opening rear door and side windows for export.
8. Full-length canvas hood with side windows for export.
9. Full-length canvas hood.
10. Chassis/cab with bonnet and wings.
11. Chassis/scuttle with bonnet and wings.

*Since the mid-1960s, Rover had taken to showing silhouette charts to illustrate the multiplicity of production-line Land Rover variants. The chart for the 109s dates from 1967; the other dates from 1968, and shows not only the 88s and 109s but the Forward Control options as well.*

### 88" REGULAR LAND-ROVER
1. Full length canvas hood
2. Full length canvas hood with side windows for export
3. Hardtop with tailboard and top hinged flap
4. Hardtop with side hinged rear door
5. Hardtop with fixed side windows (export only) tailboard and top hinged flap
6. Hardtop with fixed side windows (export only) and side hinged rear door
7. Hardtop with sliding side windows (export only) tailboard and top hinged flap
8. Hardtop with sliding side windows (export only) and side hinged rear door
9. Cab, ¾ canvas hood with side windows for export
10. Cab, ¾ canvas hood
11. Cab, open rear body
12. Chassis with cab and cab base
13. Chassis with wings, dash and seat-base

### 109" LONG LAND-ROVER
14. Cab and open rear body
15. Cab and ¾ canvas hood
16. Cab and ¾ canvas hood with side windows for export
17. Hardtop with tailboard and top hinged flap
18. Hardtop with side hinged door
19. Hardtop with tailboard and top hinged flap and fixed side windows for export
20. Hardtop with side hinged rear door and fixed side windows for export
21. Full length canvas hood with side windows for export
22. Full length canvas hood
23. Chassis with cab and cab base
24. Chassis with wings, dash and seat-base

### STATION WAGONS
25. Station wagon 7 seater
26. Station wagon 10 seater
27. Station wagon 12 seater

### 110" FORWARD CONTROL LAND-ROVER
28. Cab and fixed side rear body
29. Cab and dropside rear body
30. Cab and fixed side rear body, ¾ canvas hood
31. Cab and dropside rear body, ¾ canvas hood
32. Cab and fixed side rear body, ¾ canvas hood with side windows for export
33. Cab and drop side rear body, ¾ canvas hood with side windows for export
34. Cab and platform rear body
35. Chassis and cab with subframe*
36. Chassis and cab, no subframe*
37. Chassis with wings, dash, seat-base with subframe*
38. Chassis with wings, dash, seat-base*

### NOTE
Reference should be made to the Sales Department before any consideration is given to the use of chassis marked * above since certain limitations in their use may apply.

# POWER TAKE-OFF VERSATILITY

### HYDRAULIC SERVICES

1. The bottom power take-off can be supplied complete with an integral hydraulic pump.

2. Provision can be made to drive a variety of equipment, including winches, from the engine crankshaft.

3. The centre power take-off can be supplied complete with an integral hydraulic pump to provide the motive power for equipment such as winches.

### MECHANICAL SERVICES

4. A drive can be taken from the centre power take-off to machinery mounted below the rear body floor.

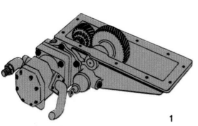
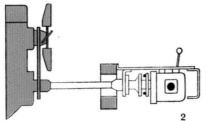

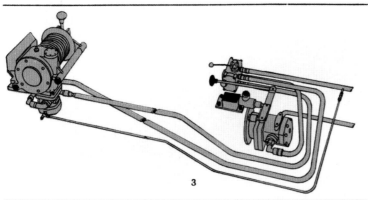

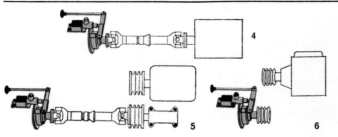

5. A drive can also be taken from the centre power take-off to an outrigger bearing mounted in the chassis frame, and then by belt to machinery mounted in the rear body section.

6. Centre power take-off equipped with V belt pulley will drive a machine mounted in place of the cab centre seat.

7. Rear power take-off equipped with a V belt pulley will drive a machine mounted in the rear body section.

8. The rear power take-off can be supplied complete with a flat belt drive unit for driving remote stationary equipment.

9. Rear power take-off driving a universal propeller shaft can be employed to operate trailer-mounted equipment, or remote stationary machinery.

**Note:** The components shown in outline, without colour, are **not** supplied by The Rover Company Limited.

*Most sales catalogues issued overseas were clones of the UK variety, translated into the local language, but Deutsche Rover in Germany produced some of their own. This one was for the Series IIA models and dated from 1963.*

*It was still important to stress the Land Rover's versatility as a workhorse, of course, and these illustrations of the various power take-off options were designed to do exactly that. They date from 1967.*

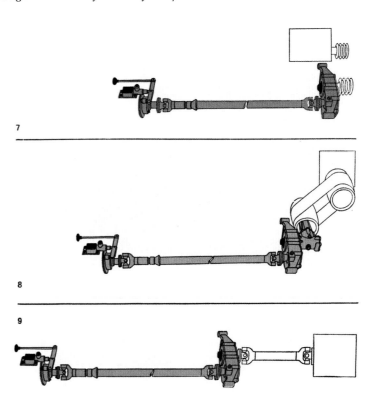

101 / LRA

# DE-LUXE SEATS

## THE ROVER COMPANY LTD
## SOLIHULL WARWICKSHIRE

Following two years of scientific design and development an alternative form of front seating is now available for Land-Rover owners requiring that extra degree of comfort and luxury.

Finished in black P.V.C. to match the existing interior trim of the Land-Rover, the de-luxe seats have fluted backrest panels and cushions, give positive body location and excellent lateral support. The centre section of each seat consists of foam latex rubber and the side rolls are of moulded polyether foam.

Apart from its superior comfort, the non-slip properties of the trim and the increased support provided offer greater safety, especially when the vehicle is used extensively on cross-country operations.

Both the driver's and outer passenger's seat are provided with fore and aft adjustment, whilst the centre seat, in matching trim, is fixed in position.

Land-Rover de-luxe seats must be specified at the time of ordering the vehicle and will then be fitted at the factory during production.

Printed in England

**FOR FURTHER INFORMATION CONSULT**

your local Land-Rover distributor or dealer, or
The Rover Co. Ltd., Technical Sales Dept.,
Lode Lane, Solihull, Birmingham, England

The Rover Company Limited reserves the right to alter specifications, colour, designs or prices without notice and without incurring any obligation. While every effort is made, in Rover literature, to provide information that is strictly up to date no responsibility can be accepted for such alterations that occur after date of going to press. Persons dealing in the Company's goods are not the agents of the Company and have no authority whatsoever to bind the Company by any expressed or implied undertaking. Sales are conditional upon terms of business, warranties and service arrangements issued by The Rover Company Limited.

*Among the accessories introduced in the later 1960s were these DeLuxe seats, which could only be fitted on the assembly lines as an extra-cost option. The outer pair had fore-and-aft adjustment (although rearward travel was limited by the centre bulkhead) and the seats were in black while the rest of the trim was grey. Similar seats were later standardised on Series III models.*

# FORWARD CONTROLS

The Forward Control models could trace their origins right back to the mid-1950s, when Rover looked at building a minibus on a forward-control version of the 107-inch chassis. By moving the driving comportment forward and over the engine, far more body space could be obtained without any increase in overall dimensions. Although this idea was abandoned, the idea of a forward-control load carrier was revived at the end of the 1950s as Land Rover began to look at expanding the Land Rover range upwards to carry larger loads.

Development took some time, and the first Forward Control model – rated to carry 30cwt (1524kg) on the road and 25 cwt (1270kg) off the road – was introduced in 1962. It used a modified 109-inch chassis, with an extra sub-frame above the rear to support the load bed, and the cab contained several recognisable Land Rover panels. However, it was immediately obvious that the Forward Control was under-developed: with the four-cylinder petrol engine, it was under-powered; it was also under-braked and prone to over-turning on steep side-slopes.

Rover swiftly followed up with a six-cylinder engine option, available for export only from late 1962, although in practice several were sold in Britain. Redevelopment brought heavy-duty ENV axles and wider tracks as well, and a slight adjustment of dimensions associated with these increased the wheelbase to 110 inches. The 110-inch model was introduced in 1966. It was also known as a Series IIB type, the earlier 109 Forward Control having been a Series IIA. This was the only use of the Series IIB name – and of course the first ones were (with typical inconsistency) actually Series IIB, Suffix A types.

The Forward Controls lasted only until 1971, when British Leyland ruled that their low volumes were no longer viable for production. In practice, the very last one was built up from parts in 1973 after a gap of two years. This was not the end of the Forward Control story, though, because many of the lessons learned from the models of the 1960s went into the special 101-inch military Forward Control that was built in the mid-1970s.

*The Forward Control was a strangely handsome-looking beast, despite its shortcomings. The red banner here is slightly misleading out of context; a diesel engine was indeed available in the normal-control models, but not in the Forward Controls at this stage. It had been planned as an option, but left the vehicle so underpowered that Rover had decided not to proceed to production.*

*This wonderfully dramatic picture on the cover of the very first Forward Control sales catalogue had all the right elements – a rugged landscape, a Land Rover cresting a steep slope, an overseas registration plate suggesting the vehicle had found users somewhere in the colonies, and a general air of action. In fact, the vehicle was one of the prototypes, pictured while being demonstrated to the South African Defence Force near Pretoria in January 1962.*

Forward Control with drop-side body.

# FORWARD CONTROL LAND-ROVER

### (AVAILABLE IN OVERSEAS MARKETS ONLY)

The Forward Control Land-Rover has been designed to combine the accepted Land-Rover four-wheel drive mobility and toughness with a carrying capacity up to twice that of the Long model. It will deal easily with a 30-cwt. payload on roads and tracks and with 25-cwt. across rough country. Its high ground clearance and excellent weight distribution make it ideal for cross-country travel. It has the same speed range as the Long Land-Rover, can climb a 1 in 2 slope fully laden and has a side tipping angle of over 40 degrees.

Although unlike other Land-Rover models in appearance, the Forward Control vehicle uses a very high percentage of standard Land-Rover parts, a fact of great significance to fleet owners. Various body styles are available.

*A very comfortable two-seater cab is provided. Heater and passenger-side windscreen wiper extra.*

*Truck-cab with fixed-side body and three-quarter length hood.*

*Truck cab with flat platform body.*

*These pictures gave a good idea of what the Forward Control was all about. There were dropside and fixed-side bodies, with or without a canvas tilt, and flatbeds as well. In practice, large numbers of Forward Controls were fitted with special bodies by approved specialist converters. The cab interior used mainly standard Land Rover parts, although the gear levers were differently – and awkwardly – placed. This is an early brochure, from the brief period in early 1963 when the Forward Controls were only available for export.*

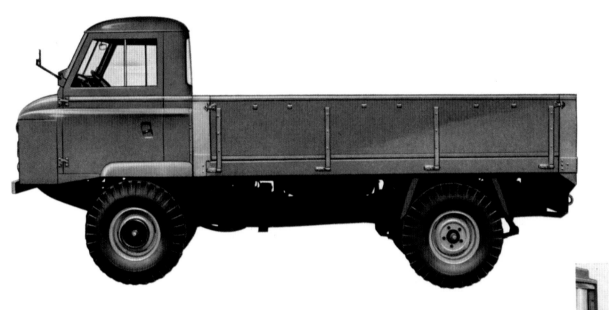

The Forward Control Land-Rover is primarily a load carrier and is available with various types of body suitable for the carriage of bulk loads and personnel. It can be supplied with a flat platform, a fixed-side body, or a drop-side body (left). A truck cab is standard equipment, but rear seats and hoods are also available.

The Forward Control Land-Rover is the most recent addition to the multifarious Land-Rover family. Based on the Long, 109 inch wheelbase, chassis it is able to cope easily with a 30-cwt. payload on roads and country tracks and with a 25-cwt. payload across the roughest terrain. It has been designed to combine the accepted Land-Rover four-wheel drive mobility and robustness with a load capacity up to twice that of the Long Land-Rover. Because it has larger tyres (9·00 × 16 in.), a greater ground clearance (10 in.), and a better weight distribution between the axles, the cross-country performance of the Forward Control is exceptionally good. It has the same speed range as the Long Land-Rover, can climb a gradient of 1 in 2 when fully laden and has a side tipping angle of over 40 degrees.

*Heater and passenger-side windscreen wiper extra.*

The standard colour for the Forward Control was the Mid-Grey already available on normal-control models and far lighter than this catalogue illustration suggested.

The most obvious recognition feature of the Series IIB or 110-inch Forward Control was the repositioned headlamps, now directly above the bumper. The change had been brought about by lighting regulations overseas, and it appears that some of the later 109-inch Forward Controls for Switzerland and possibly also Germany and Austria were built with the revised front end.

The controls had been redesigned for the 110-inch model, with a longer handbrake that the driver could reach while wearing a seat belt (though belts were not yet compulsory) and a relocated gearchange with a more positive feel. Even then, the Forward Control's gearchange was not among the best.

This picture from the 110-inch Forward Control catalogue gives a good idea of the model's strength. Buyers could get 30cwt in there, and the flat floor had no wheel arch intrusions. Not immediately obvious in this picture is that there was nevertheless an intrusion into the load area. At front centre of the load bed there was a "box", which when removed gave access to the engine.

LAND-ROVER

110" WHEELBASE
FORWARD
CONTROL

*In flat-bed form, the Forward Control offered a long load bed that was ideal for tasks such as the timber clearance pictured here.*

*Moody and magnificent ... well, perhaps not, but the picture made a good cover for the Forward Control catalogue in 1967.*

*This was the chassis of the 110-inch Forward Control. The rear axle was mounted under the springs, but the front axle was above them. The extra sub-frame that carried the body is clear here, and the new long handbrake, revised gearchange control, and front anti-roll bar can all be seen more clearly than would have been possible in an ordinary photograph.*

**TRANSMISSION**
Two- or four-wheel drive. Main gearbox has four forward speeds and one reverse with synchromesh on third and top. Two additional ratios are provided in the transfer box giving a total of eight forward and two reverse speeds. This wide speed range combined with the vehicle's other features enables all kinds of terrain to be traversed. Front and rear axles are fully-floating and have spiral bevel drive.

**CHASSIS FRAME**
Welded steel box-section of great strength, with body subframe. Box-section cross-members give torsional and diagonal rigidity.

**ENGINES**
Four-cylinder diesel and six-cylinder petrol for home market. Four-cylinder petrol also available for export.

**POWER TAKE-OFF**
Provision for centre power take-off to drive a pump, compressor, generator or under-body-mounted winch.

**BRAKES**
Hydraulic, with servo assistance. Two leading shoes on front. Transmission-type handbrake.

**SUSPENSION**
Semi-elliptic springs, overslung at rear, controlled by double-acting hydraulic telescopic shock absorbers.

**BODY**
All body panels of non-corrodible light alloy. External steel fittings are heavily galvanised.

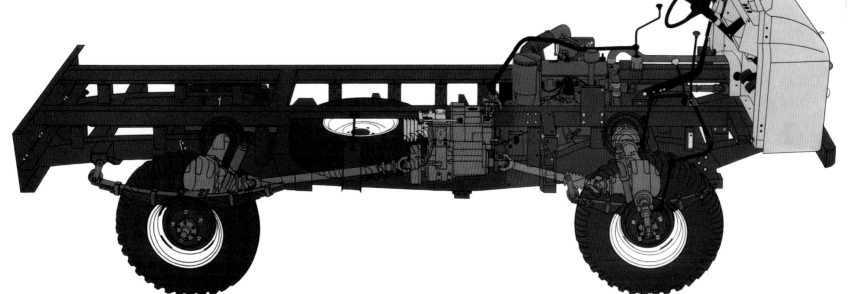

*Action photography was increasingly favoured by the time of the 1967 sales catalogue.*

The 110″ Forward Control Land-Rover is an outstanding cross-country vehicle which combines the accepted 4-wheel drive mobility of the smaller models with a greater load capacity. The latest version has increased track, a specially designed anti-roll bar, heavy-duty axle assemblies, wider spring bases and stronger springs, mounted over the axles at the rear—all developments adding up to greater stability and strength.

1. Fixed side body.
2. Dropside body.
3. Fixed side body with canvas hood.
4. Dropside body with canvas hood.
5. Fixed side body with canvas hood and side windows for export.
6. Dropside body with canvas hood and side windows for export.
7. Platform body.
8. Chassis cab with subframe.
9. Chassis cab without subframe.
10. Chassis with wings, dash, seat-base and sub-frame.
11. Chassis with wings, dash, seat-base, without subframe.

*There were 11 different types of Forward Control available from the assembly lines. Just in case it wasn't obvious, the catalogue also showed how useful a standard platform or flat-bed model could be around the farm.*

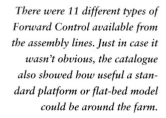

# OVERSEAS – AND ESPECIALLY IN AMERICA

Exports accounted for the lion's share of Land Rover production, but in many of the territories where the vehicles were sold, there was no call for sales catalogues because sales were made to government agencies and large corporations, not through showrooms to individuals. In countries where there was a need for sales catalogues, such as in Europe, the local importers very often made use of the standard UK catalogue with the text replaced by a translated version. There were nevertheless some catalogues specially prepared outside the UK.

The major exception was North America. Land Rovers were sold in both Canada and the USA, and selling Land Rovers in the home of the Jeep was always an uphill struggle. In 1962, Rover made a determined push to crack the US market with both Land Rovers and Rover cars, and an innovative new team at Rover North America came up with some eye-catching publicity materials. That team was also not afraid to point out to Solihull that Land Rovers were simply underpowered for US expectations.

One result was a special 109 Station Wagon for what Rover called the North American Dollar Area (NADA) in 1966; the other was that Rover bought the manufacturing and development rights to a General Motors (Buick) alloy V8 engine in 1965. Originally intended only for Land Rovers in the USA, the engine was so good that it was diverted to Rover cars – and Land Rovers did not get it until 1978. By that time, there were no Land Rovers for the USA; Rover had pulled out in 1974 in the face of slow sales and increasing safety and emissions regulations.

There were special circumstances in Spain, too, where Metalurgica de Santa Ana (trading as Santana) had been assembling Land Rovers from CKD kits since 1958. Its first vehicles were Series II models, and had no significant differences from the Solihull-built type. However, the Spanish government had only allowed the assembly operation to be set up on condition that it made progress towards full local manufacture as well as assembly.

By 1967, Santana had achieved that aim, and in that year it also introduced the first model to its own design. Though broadly similar to its Land Rover equivalent, the 1300

**Basic Facts**

Land-Rovers have been travelling the roads and working the rough lands of the world for nearly twenty years. Today, they still lead the field in virtually every aspect of 4-wheel drive operation. Outwardly, the Land-Rover has changed little in ten years simply because its practical design and rugged construction are best suited to the enormous diversity of jobs it is called upon to do. Mechanically, however, a great many developments have progressively taken place to improve the breed and keep pace with the special and ever-growing needs of operators all over the world. The modern Land-Rover represents an important advance over its counterparts of only a few years ago. With a choice of petrol or diesel engine, short or long chassis, bonneted or forward control, 38 body styles, an extensive range of optional equipment, including special-purpose tyres, and appliances and bodies by approved manufacturers, it is now, more than ever, The World's Most Versatile Vehicle.

model was a Forward Control model on the 109-inch chassis that had a lower loading height than the Solihull model because it lacked the additional frame above the chassis. It also had a different cab design and a lower load capacity of 1300kg, from which the name was taken. As time went on, Santana Land Rovers began to differ more and more from the Solihull product, although they retained the Land Rover name and badging until Santana and Land Rover parted company in 1990.

*This picture of Land Rovers lined up on a dockside in the 1960s was used to remind potential buyers that the vehicles were a huge export success and were in use all over the world.*

Photographs had a particular value in illustrating the Land Rover's use overseas, because in those days there was a general belief that they could not be falsified. These pictures from a mid-1960s sales catalogue show examples at work in Abu Dhabi and on a construction site closer to home.

In the USA, the target customer was the outdoorsman, and this specially-shot cover picture was used on a 1962 catalogue for the Series IIA. Inside, however, the illustrations were the same as in contemporary UK catalogues.

Rover also ran an Overseas Delivery scheme, which allowed visitors to the UK to take delivery of a new Rover or Land Rover at the factory in Solihull. The Station Wagon illustration is supposed to set the tone, with the background being a railway terminal in Germany.

ROVER OVERSEAS VISITORS DELIVERY SCHEME

**BEST 4-WHEEL DRIVE**

**VEHICLE IN THE WORLD**

*Rover North America told showroom visitors that the Land Rover was the best four-wheel drive vehicle in the world, but a nation proud of inventing the Jeep was not inclined to believe that.*

*The new team at RNA tried shock tactics. This remarkable sales brochure was prepared for a motor show in the USA in April 1963 – at Easter time, so it was in the shape of an Easter egg. There were similar catalogues for Rover cars as well. The inside pages were more prosaic.*

**STATION WAGONS
HARD TOPS
OPEN OR CANVAS TOPS** } ALL EQUIPPED WITH
4-WHEEL DRIVE AND
A LOW RANGE OF GEARS
—STANDARD!

ALUMINUM ALLOY BODY—will not rust

FITTINGS GALVANIZED—for protection

HEAVY BOX FRAME—(look at it)—for strength

HIGH GEAR RANGE and REAR WHEEL DRIVE—for open road cruising

LOW GEAR RANGE—for climbing, descending, or going through slush

4-WHEEL DRIVE—for still more traction

FAMOUS ROVER
DIESEL ENGINE
ALSO AVAILABLE
( cheaper than brand X !)

The Land Rover has a great deal of equipment as standard and at no extra charge because The Rover Company thinks you need it.

**THE ROVER MOTOR COMPANY OF NORTH AMERICA LIMITED**

405 LEXINGTON AVE. NEW YORK, N.Y. 10017     373 SHAW ROAD. SO. SAN FRANCISCO. CALIF. 94080
1040 BAYVIEW DR., FT. LAUDERDALE. FLA. 33304     10889 WILSHIRE BLVD., LOS ANGELES. CALIF. 90024

MOBILE DRIVE. TORONTO 16. ONT.     156 W. SECOND AVE., VANCOUVER 10. B.C.

*Characteristic of RNA advertising in the early 1960s was a dry sense of humour. Here it is in the box about the diesel engine, which is claimed to be "cheaper than Brand X".*

105

# LAND - ROVER

- ALUMINUM ALLOY NON-RUST BODY
- BOX SECTION FRAME—extra heavy
- FULLY FLOATING AXLES
- OIL BATH AIR CLEANER—standard
- 8 FORWARD SPEEDS—2 REVERSE
- FULL FLOW OIL FILTER—standard
- GASOLINE OR DIESEL ENGINE

- HEAT SHIELD ROOF
- 3 POWER TAKE-OFF POINTS
- ALL METAL RUST-PROOFED
- 6-PLY TIRES—standard
- FULL TOOL KIT—standard
- ALL FITTINGS GALVANIZED
- ONLY TWO GREASE POINTS

- 108 PIECES OPTIONAL EQUIPMENT (Snow ploughs, mowers, winches, etc.)
- TWO CHASSIS LENGTHS AVAILABLE
- 10 BODY STYLES
- CANVAS TOP OR HARD TOP
- 7, 10, or 12 PASSENGER STATION WAGONS
- POWERFUL KODIAK HEATER
- Built by one of England's oldest and largest automobile makers
- Costs no more than an ordinary four-wheel drive vehicle

## GREENWICH AUTOMOBILES, inc.

240 Mason Street,          Greenwich, Conn.

Mr. Werner Wagner, President

203 TO 9-6666

*Even the US dealers got in on the act. This one in Greenwich, Connecticut, pictured "his" Land Rover leaping into the air, while "hers" contrived to look almost dainty.*

*The "powerful Kodiak heater" was a Canadian-made extra not available outside North America which went some way to overcoming one of the Land Rover's most obvious failings in some of the continent's extreme climates.*

# LAND - ROVER
# KODIAK MK III
## FRESH - AIR HEATER

FIG.1

THE ROVER MOTOR COMPANY OF NORTH AMERICA LIMITED now introduces the Kodiak Mark 111 Fresh Air Heater, a further development of the Land-Rover heater, with increased heating and de-icing capacity, plus improved air circulation, which is designed and built in Canada for applications in extreme winter conditions. This rugged, efficient unit is now being supplied by Land-Rover dealers throughout North America.

Large defrost outlets provide full and efficient defrosting. The trunking has been designed with passenger comfort and leg room in mind. In addition to the normal air flow to the passenger's feet, a further outlet is provided for and controllable by the passenger.

FIG.2

FIG.3

The control of the two speed electric motor and the coolant flow is effected by two push-pull switches mounted on the dash panel in front of the driver.

Output------------------17,500 B.T.U.s/hr.
Air Flow--------------------- 190 C.F.M.

## THE ROVER MOTOR COMPANY
### OF NORTH AMERICA LIMITED

MOBILE DRIVE·TORONTO 16·ONTARIO
156 WEST SECOND AVENUE·VANCOUVER 10·B C
DOMINION SQUARE BUILDING · MONTREAL 2 · QUE.

405 LEXINGTON AVENUE · NEW YORK 17 · N Y
36-12 37TH STREET·LONG ISLAND CITY · N Y
373 SHAW ROAD·SOUTH SAN FRANCISCO CALIFORNIA

*Perhaps taking their cue from Rover's earlier use of attractive hand-produced illustrations, RNA had some of their own done, showing typical North American scenes. These two were used in a calendar sent out to favoured individuals in 1965. The nearest picture shows an interesting box-like structure mounted at the rear. This may have been a locally-made optional extra.*

Layout of instruments and controls in the new series II A 109" Land-Rover Station Wagon with 160 cubic inch 6 cylinder engine.

**THE 6 CYLINDER LONG WHEELBASE STATION WAGON** adds to the world-renowned rugged qualities of the Land-Rover a high cruising speed capability on the open road.

To cope with the increased performance of the 6 cylinder engine, servo assisted brakes have been added.

Standard equipment includes 8 forward, 2 reverse speeds, limited slip differential rear axle.

## SIX CYLINDER STATION WAGON

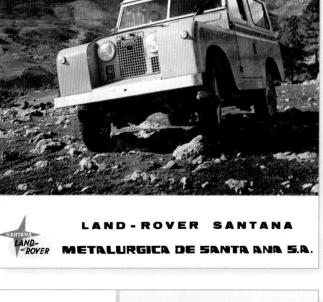

LAND-ROVER SANTANA
METALURGICA DE SANTA ANA S.A.

From summer 1966, US and Canadian buyers had their own special version of the 109 Station Wagon. Not only did it have the 2.6-litre six-cylinder engine unavailable elsewhere in normal-control models, but that engine was the high-compression Rover car type which gave extra road performance. The NADA (North American Dollar Area) Station Wagon also had its own dash, with large demister vents and a new three-spoke steering wheel.

LAND-ROVER SANTANA, MODELO 1300

*Santana's own Forward Control, the 1300 model, had a number of important differences from the equivalent Solihull product of the time.*

*In the beginning, Spanish-assembled Land Rovers were very simply that, although there was a special badge that read "Land Rover Santana". These are Series IIA models from the early 1960s.*

*The Spanish-built Santana 88 Station Wagons had this interesting front-end arrangement by 1970, with four headlamps. Their 109 equivalents nevertheless stuck to two.*

# REGULATIONS

After the middle of the 1960s, new regulations about the configuration of road vehicles began to proliferate around the world. The rot had set in after Ralph Nader's Unsafe At Any Speed diatribe against the shortcomings of the US motor industry. Within a couple of years, there were regulations about everything from safety belts to exhaust emissions, and the problem for the motor manufacturers was that different countries began to want different things.

On the Land Rover side of the house, the first big issue for Solihull affected headlamp positions. Traditionally, the Land Rover's headlamps had been set alongside the radiator grille in a panel that was set back to protect them as much as possible from flying stones and errant tree branches. However, in the brave new world of the late 1960s, this was no longer good enough. From 1 January 1969, Land Rovers sold in the USA had to conform to new regulations which demanded that the headlamps should be nearer to the outer extremities of the vehicle. The Benelux countries – Belgium, the Netherlands and Luxembourg – were in full agreement that this was a good idea, and introduced their own new

legislation that insisted on it.

Solihull's first reaction was simply to move the headlamps out to the wing fronts. This was hardly a novel solution, as it had been adopted for some special conversions, such as the air conditioning installation by Normalair, that needed the full width of the grille panel for other purposes. The "production" version added a new grille panel without cutouts for the headlamps, and a redesigned wire-mesh grille in the shape of a square with a lump at the top. This was something of a stop-gap solution, but it was introduced on the production lines late in 1968 for vehicles destined for those countries where the new legislation applied. For other countries, including the UK, the original design remained in place for the time being.

Stuck out on the wing fronts, the headlamps were not only vulnerable, but also looked odd. American buyers quickly christened these thankfully short-lived models "Bug-eye" types for fairly obvious reasons. Meanwhile, a long-term solution was in hand at Solihull. The wing fronts were carefully redesigned to allow the headlamps to be recessed into them for greater protection. The cut-out was shaped to allow a hand to grip the headlamp unit and unscrew it for easy replacement (as was required on British military vehicles). On civilian models, the octagonal cut-out was concealed by a finisher panel in front of the wing and afforded even more protection to the headlamp. There was a new wire-mesh grille, too, in the shape of a cross rather than the traditional inverted T. The new design entered production in April 1969, but it did not turn the Series IIA models into Series IIB types, as so many people seem to think. All that happened was a change of chassis suffix letter from F to G.

## FOR EXTRA HEAVY DUTY

Powered by the 6-cylinder, 2·6 Litre petrol engine, the 109″ wheelbase 1-Ton Land-Rover supplements the already extensive range of Land-Rover vehicles and it has been developed to meet the demands of operators who require a greater load-carrying capacity than is offered by the normal 109″ Land-Rover.

With an increase of a ¼-ton in cross-country payload capacity the 1-Ton Land-Rover is, of course, equipped with a more rugged specification. Features include heavy-duty axles and suspension, servo-assisted brakes that ensure an ample safety margin under all conditions, larger tyres to cope with load increase and to induce greater floatation on soft ground and a lower-ratio steering box. To minimise any steering wheel reaction which may be encountered over rough terrain, a hydraulic steering damper is fitted as standard.

Low speed performance is maintained by the use of lower transfer box ratios, whilst a maximum speed in top gear of over 60 m.p.h. is still attainable for normal road use.

The introduction of this 1-Ton model adds to the already wide-ranging character of the Land-Rover and makes it more than ever, the world's most versatile vehicle.

**1969 LAND-ROVER**

SUGGESTED RETAIL PRICE AT EAST COAST PORTS OF ENTRY — $3,295.00

SUGGESTED RETAIL PRICE AT WEST COAST PORTS OF ENTRY — $3,360.00

The original sales catalogue was replaced at the start of the 1969 model-year in autumn 1968 with one that showed the One Ton as it really was. Few were ordered as truck cab types like this one, though, and in practice the One Ton chassis was favoured as the basis of special conversions that required its heavier payload. One Tons had the "drop-shackle" suspension originally developed for the military so that they could run on larger 9.00 x 16 tyres. They also had altered transfer box gearing and a number of other detail differences from standard 109s.

The "Bug-eye" models didn't last long enough to feature in new sales catalogues in Europe, but Rover North America thought it was important to offer catalogues that showed the vehicles as they really were – even if the latest appearance was only temporary. Perhaps they were afraid that somebody would sue them for misrepresentation if they didn't; American buyers were rather good at that kind of thing. So this was a 1969 Land Rover as far as the USA was concerned. The vent in the wing is for the Kodiak heater that was available only in North America; it was manufactured in Canada and fitted in the USA.

Farmyard scenes still sold Land Rovers, and one of the new 88s was pictured for sales material in a typical setting – now with horses rather than the cows seen a couple of years ago. This is the cover of the German-language edition, identical to the English one in all but language.

The Rover Company was still targeting its traditional Land Rover customers. This 1969-model 109 was posed looking suspiciously clean on a muddy construction site, and then picked up a tilt cover for a little forestry work. All the early publicity vehicles had those DXC-G registrations.

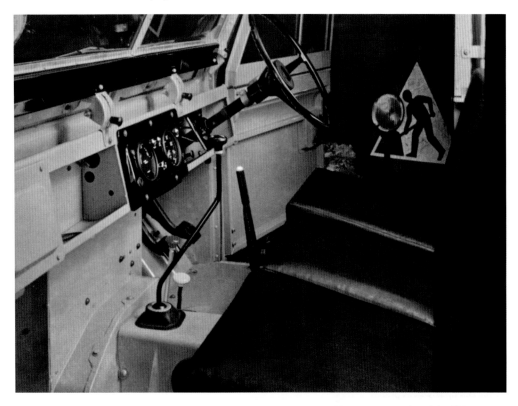

*Left. Cab of the four-cylinder petrol-engined Land-Rover. Left-hand steering is also available.*

The truck cab on both four-cylinder and six-cylinder models offers all-round visibility for driver and two passengers, with the added convenience of an adjustable driving seat. Instruments and switches are grouped centrally and include a water temperature gauge and combined ignition/starter switch. An extended handbrake lever ensures ease of application by a driver wearing a safety harness.

Heating, de-luxe seats, special trim and other cab refinements can be provided as optional extras.

The rear body space will take an endless variety of loads up to a limit of 2,000 lb. (908 kg.) on roads or 1,800 lb. (816 kg.) across rough country. Its aluminium alloy construction is non-rusting and anti-corrosive. The spare wheel is normally mounted at the side of the body but an alternative bonnet mounting can be fitted as an extra.

*Below, left. Six-cylinder petrol-engined Land-Rover cab shown. The comfortable and smart de-luxe seats are an optional extra. Left-hand steering also available.*

*The cab of a Land Rover was still a pretty spartan place, as the upper picture here makes clear. By comparison, the pleated seats, floor trim and door cards of the optional DeLuxe cab shown below do seem deserving of the name. There is even a heater, just visible hanging under the dashboard near the centre. The cranked gear lever was used on four-cylinder models; the straight lever belonged to six-cylinder 109s, and was mounted slightly further back.*

### 4-cylinder diesel engine

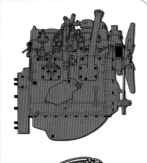

Diesel power is available and adds further to the efficiency and economy of the Land-Rover in working conditions which favour the use of this type of engine. A rugged 2¼-litre, four cylinder unit, the Rover diesel engine develops a maximum of 62 b.h.p. (DIN) at 4,000 rev/min, and maximum torque of 14·2 Mkg (102·7 lb.ft.) at 1,800 rev/min. This unit is particularly suitable for stationary P.T.O. applications having an inbuilt governor and a hand throttle as standard equipment. The standard four-bladed fan on the diesel engine is sufficient for the usual power take-off applications.

### 6-cylinder petrol engine

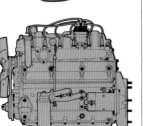

The 2·6-litre six-cylinder petrol engine is standard in 1-Ton models, and is offered as an alternative in the Long Land-Rover. Its greater capacity provides an increased power output for those users whose operations call for above average road work. Compression ratios of 7·8 to 1 and 7 to 1 are available, the latter for use in territories where petrol with octane ratings of under 85 only are obtainable. With the former, 86 b.h.p. (DIN) is developed at 4,500 rev/min, with 18·2 Mkg (131·6 lb.ft.) torque at 1,750 rev/min.

### 4-cylinder petrol engine

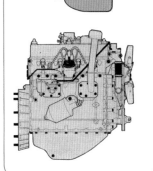

The four-cylinder, 2¼-litre petrol engine is a well-proved unit of outstanding reliability that has powered many millions of Land-Rover miles. Introduced with the Series II Land-Rover in 1958 this engine has been steadily developed so that with its present compression ratio of 8·0 : 1 it develops a maximum of 70·5 b.h.p. (DIN) at 4,000 rev/min, with maximum torque of 16·5 Mkg (119·3 lb.ft.) at 1,500 rev/min. It has overhead valves operated by rockers and push rods, with roller type cam-followers, and has an over-square bore/stroke ratio with dimensions of 90·47 mm and 88·9 mm.

*Unusually, this May 1971 sales catalogue called the 88 truck cab model a ½-ton Pick-Up. Somebody was getting lazy, though: the picture shows one of the first Series IIAs with lights in the wings, built in 1968. There was no attempt even to alter the registration suffix with an airbrush to make the vehicle look newer.*

*At the end of Series IIA production in 1971, the engines were the ones they had been since 1967. They were a four-cylinder 2¼-litre diesel, a similar four-cylinder petrol, and a 2.6-litre six-cylinder petrol.*

**109 in. Long**

**88 in. Regular**

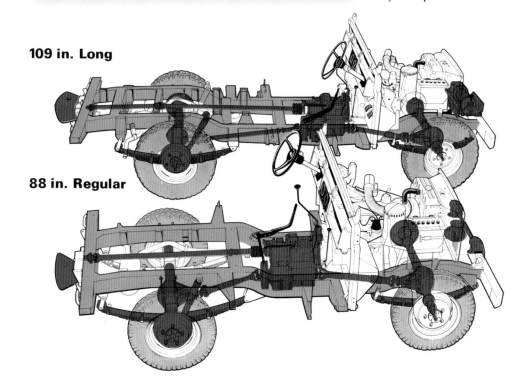

*Again, this catalogue dates from May 1971, but the drawings all show earlier vehicles, though at least of the right general specification. Either the money or the will was not available to alter the registration suffixes to bring the drawings up to date.*

*Altering the colours on the drawings could not disguise the fact that the drawings had been seen before, or that neither 88 nor 109 had changed significantly in recent years.*

# SPECIAL PROJECTS

The Special Projects Department was kept very busy from its inception in 1957 right through until 1981, when it was reorganised after the retirement of its long-term head, George Mackie. The department's golden age was the 1960s, however, when conversions of all kinds and equipment of all shapes and sizes were submitted for testing and approval.

The department dealt with pretty much anything and everything that was not or could not be fitted on the main assembly lines. So special bodies for fire appliances and ambulances fell into the Special Projects remit. There were more ambitious conversions, too, such as the tractor-wheeled Roadless and tracked Cuthbertson conversions, and a variety of less major conversions such as snow ploughs, refuse collectors, recovery cranes and campers. The list was then topped off by what were really glorified accessories, such as free-

**THE REDWING LAND-ROVER FIRE APPLIANCE TYPE FT/1 AND FT/2**

As approved by The ROVER CO. LTD.

**REDWING FT/1**
based on
88″ REGULAR LAND-ROVER

Accommodation for crew of three in driving compartment

¾ Rear View (without cab)

**REDWING FT/2**
based on
109″ LONG LAND-ROVER

Accommodation for crew of five; three in the driving compartment, two in rear of appliance

¾ Rear View (with cab)

CARMICHAEL & SONS (Worcester) LIMITED

**THE REDWING LAND-ROVER FIRE APPLIANCE TYPE FT/3 AND FT/4**

As approved by The ROVER CO. LTD.

**REDWING FT/3**
based on
109″ LONG LAND-ROVER

Fully open bodywork

¾ Rear View

*Carmichael's seem to have been the first to gain Land Rover Approval for their fire appliance conversions, and in the first half of the 1960s they built up a wide range of types. All were known by the brand name of Redwing, and all carried an FT type prefix – which presumably stood for Fire Tender. These leaflets show the five varieties available on standard normal-control chassis.*

**REDWING FT/4**
based on
109″ LONG LAND-ROVER

Open rear body
Fully enclosed cab.
Accommodation for crew of five on both these models; three in the driving compartment, two in rear of appliance.

View to show control panel

CARMICHAEL & SONS (Worcester) LIMITED

**THE REDWING LAND-ROVER FIRE APPLIANCE TYPE FT/5**

As approved by The ROVER CO. LTD.

**REDWING FT/5**
109″ LONG LAND-ROVER

In road condition, shutters closed.

Appliance specially equipped to customers' requirements

Appliance with shutters down showing ease of access to internally stowed equipment. Accommodation for crew of five on both these models; three in the driving compartment, two in rear of appliance.

Appliance specially equipped to customers' requirements

CARMICHAEL & SONS (Worcester) LIMITED

**HCB ANGUS FIREFLY**
400 G.P.M. FIRE ENGINE
STD 400 11 65
LAND-ROVER
APPROVED BY THE ROVER COMPANY LIMITED

**GENERAL DESCRIPTION**
This Firefly Land Rover fire appliance has been developed to satisfy the needs of both Industrial and Local Authority Fire Brigades where a compact small Fire Appliance is required.
The unit is based on the standard Land Rover chassis cab, built to a special Home or Export fire appliance specification and in its basic form offers:
Seating in standard crew cab for driver and two crew.
40-90 gallons (182-409 litres) of water, dependent upon the total ancillary equipment to be carried.
Rear mounted fire pump of 350-400 g.p.m. (1590-1816 litres per minute) output.
First aid hose reel.
Stowage for ladder and two 10ft suctions on roof gallows.
Transverse locker and two side lockers for stowage of hose, etc., with additional stowing space for small equipment, extinguishers, etc., on the rear deck within the vehicle's total capacity.

**HCB-ANGUS LTD**
HEAD OFFICE AND WORKS
**TOTTON · SOUTHAMPTON**
Phone: TOTTON 3641 (3 lines)          Telegrams: HACABO, TOTTON

**HCB ANGUS FIREFLY**
HARD-TOP FIRE ENGINE
STD DEL 11 65
LAND-ROVER
APPROVED BY THE ROVER COMPANY LIMITED

**GENERAL DESCRIPTION**
This Land Rover fire appliance has been developed as a completely enclosed unit. Being based on the standard Land Rover 'hard top' vehicle enables us to offer a first class practical fire engine at the lowest possible cost, and in its basic form offers:
Seating in cab for driver and passenger (with additional seat either side at the rear of the body if required).
40-90 galls. (182-409 litres) of water dependent upon the total ancillary equipment to be carried.
An amidships mounted 350-400 g.p.m. (1590-1816 litres per minute) fire pump or a high pressure fog pump.
One first aid hose reel.
Stowage for a ladder and 2 x 10ft. suction hoses on the roof.
A large locker each side for hose, with additional stowage space inside the rear body for small equipment.

**HCB-ANGUS LTD**
HEAD OFFICE AND WORKS
**TOTTON · SOUTHAMPTON**
Phone: TOTTON 3641 (3 lines)          Telegrams: HACABO, TOTTON

**HCB ANGUS FIREFLY**
HI-FOG FIRE ENGINE
STD HP 11 65
LAND-ROVER
APPROVED BY THE ROVER COMPANY LIMITED

**GENERAL DESCRIPTION**
This Land Rover fire engine has been developed for use as a general purpose high efficiency first aid unit giving up to 500 p.s.i. high pressure or 75 g.p.m. (340 litres per minute) at 75 p.s.i. volume output.
The unit is based on the standard Land Rover chassis cab to a special home or export fire appliance specification and in its basic form offers:
Seating in the standard crew cab for driver and two crew.
80 gall. (363 litres) water tank.
Rear mounted (Hathaway) high pressure fog pump.
Two high pressure first aid hose reels, each with 180ft high pressure hose and trigger operated Angus Fire Armour Super Fog Gun.
Stowage for two 10ft lengths of 3" suction on bonnet.
Two rear lockers for hose or small equipment.

**HCB-ANGUS LTD**
HEAD OFFICE AND WORKS
**TOTTON · SOUTHAMPTON**
Phone: TOTTON 3641 (3 lines)          Telegrams: HACABO, TOTTON

*George Angus had been a supplier of fire equipment for Land Rovers for many years, and in the early 1960s bought out Fire Armour Ltd, who built complete appliances. From 1963 the company was absorbed into Hampshire Coach Bodies and the company was renamed HCB-Angus. It developed a number of fire tender conversions for Land Rovers, and these included some that were adaptable as airfield first-response crash tenders as well. All were branded Firefly types, a name originally associated with Fire Armour.*

wheeling hubs and special seats.

Rover drew up a standardised format for sales leaflets about "approved" conversions and equipment, although not all the converters adhered to it all the time, and there was in any case considerable latitude within the basic format. Typically, the leaflets were made to a standard page size, and featured green bands across the top and bottom, although fire appliances often had red or orange bands. British Leyland were less strict about the format than Rover had been, and in the 1970s the special format began to disappear as the companies involved chose their own ways of presenting their products.

The one-man, anywhere, any weather
**PRECISION FERTILISER DISTRIBUTOR**
for use on the Series II Long Land Rover (Diesel or Petrol)

*Kenwall built their "approved" fertiliser distributor on a 109 chassis-cab.*

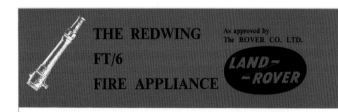

## THE REDWING FT/6 FIRE APPLIANCE

As approved by The ROVER CO. LTD.

**LAND-ROVER**

*Threequarter Front View*

- Based on the 109″ Land-Rover chassis converted to Forward Control by Carmichael & Sons (Worcester) Ltd.
- Seating for crew of four.
- Choice of Fire Pumps
- 140 gallon Water Tank.
- Fully enclosed Crew and Equipment Space.
- Fibreglass Roof, Waterproof, Rustproof.
- Four-door Cab for ease of entry and exit.
- Conversion makes the maximum use of Standard Land-Rover parts.

**CARMICHAEL & SONS (Worcester) LIMITED**

## THE REDWING TYPE FT/7 FIRE APPLIANCE

As approved by The ROVER CO. LTD.

**LAND-ROVER**

- Designed for 'off the road' conditions with large entry and exit angles and ground clearance.
- Rearward facing crew seats for safety.
- Transverse locker for equipment—large Hose Lockers.
- 150-gallon First Aid Tank.
- Easily removable water tank and mechanical components.
- Large 'working' roof area.
- Stowage for four lengths of 4 in. suction hose and up to 35-foot ladder.

ALL ENQUIRIES SHOULD BE ADDRESSED TO
**CARMICHAEL & SONS (WORCESTER) LTD. GREGORY'S MILL STREET . WORCESTER**
Telephone: WORCESTER 21393 (2 lines)

*There were also forward-control Redwing fire tenders. The FT/6 was a Carmichael "special", providing a low-height appliance within almost the same footprint as a standard 109; Carmichael's did the chassis conversion themselves, as well as building the body. Where height wasn't a problem, they also built fire tenders on the factory-supplied Forward Control chassis under the type name of FT/7.*

## Pyrene protects   Land-Rover fire appliances

The Pyrene range of Land Rover fire appliances are available for fire risks requiring Water, Dry Powder, or Foam and thus are suitable for all fire classification.

Fast, highly mobile and manoeuvrable, these appliances are ideally suited for airfields operating light aircraft or industrial concerns requiring a compact and efficient force.

Pyrene Land-Rover fire appliances are built on the regular, long and 1 ton chassis, and a standard range of optional equipment is available including a 10ft 6in/18ft 9in (3.20m/5.94m) light alloy extension ladder, suction hose and strainers, delivery hose, branchpipes, cab operated searchlights, etc.

Special attention is paid to accessibility for maintenance, and all external metal fittings are chromium plated or appropriately protected against corrosion.

**Sales and service**

Matters relating to sales, service or warranty should be addressed to our Fire Engineering Division, who will be pleased to supply any further information required concerning Pyrene Land-Rover fire appliances.

## SUN 'PURPOSE DESIGNED' FIRE APPLIANCES

As approved by The ROVER CO. LTD.

**LAND-ROVER**

### SUN BLR. 1.
based on 109′ w/b
**LAND-ROVER**
standard truck

Seating for crew of five. Water capacity 50/100 galls. SUN-HT Mk. IB. 500/600 g.p.m. pump or similar alternative

Extinguishing media- Water, Fog, Foam, CO$_2$, or Vapourising liquids.

First Aid Hosereel.

SPECIFICATION OVERLEAF

**SUN ENGINEERING (RICHMOND) LTD.
BROWELL'S LANE, FELTHAM, MIDDLESEX.**
PHONE: FELTHAM 6401     CABLES: SUNENG. HOUNSLOW.

*Carmichael's and HCB-Angus had the lion's share of the Land Rover fire tender market, but that didn't stop others from trying. Pyrene and Sun both gained approval for their conversions in the first half of the 1960s. Pyrene bought out the Sun interests in the later 1960s and continued to develop them, using the BLR type-codes of the original manufacturer.*

## TWO STRETCHER AMBULANCE

As approved by the Rover Co. Ltd. for use with the . . .

**LAND-ROVER**

THIS up-to-date ambulance incorporates the latest aluminium alloy construction techniques to combine toughness with comfort, and has all the mobility and tenacity afforded by a four-wheel drive.

The design provides for two stretchers and an attendant, one stretcher and three sitting cases, or six sitting cases.

Features include built-in wash basin with water supply, fully insulated body for tropical use, and adequate locker accommodation.

### by PILCHERS AMBULANCE BUILDERS
314, KINGSTON ROAD, WIMBLEDON, S.W.20   Telephone : LIBerty 2350 & 7058

---

**pilchers**

As approved by the Rover Co. Ltd. for use with the . . .

**LAND-ROVER**

### AMBULANCE - MODEL 7428/S2

**STANDARD MODEL**

The latest model of this popular conversion incorporates improved sealing and increased use of plastics, making for a tougher and even more efficient unit.

In retaining the same departure angle as the standard Land Rover, Pilchers have ensured the best possible performance for off-the-road ambulance operation.

### PILCHERS (MERTON) LTD.
AMBULANCE SPECIALISTS

CABLES "AMBULAP"   VICTORIA ROAD, BURGESS HILL, SUSSEX.   TELEPHONE BURGESS HILL 5707

---

*Pilcher's were long-established ambulance specialists when they turned to Land Rovers in the late 1950s. Their designs ranged from an expensive coachbuilt body down to a simple hardtop that could be fitted onto a truck cab 109.*

---

*Lomas* AMBULANCES

**LAND-ROVER**

APPROVED BY THE ROVER COMPANY LIMITED

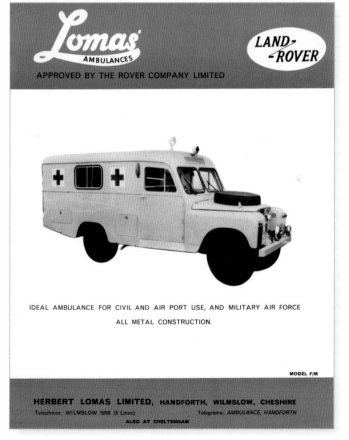

IDEAL AMBULANCE FOR CIVIL AND AIR PORT USE, AND MILITARY AIR FORCE
ALL METAL CONSTRUCTION.

MODEL F/M

### HERBERT LOMAS LIMITED, HANDFORTH, WILMSLOW, CHESHIRE
Telephone: WILMSLOW 5258 (5 Lines)   Telegrams: AMBULANCE, HANDFORTH
ALSO AT CHELTENHAM

---

*Lomas* AMBULANCES

**LAND-ROVER**

APPROVED BY THE ROVER COMPANY LIMITED

LOMAS JUNIOR DUAL PURPOSE AMBULANCE
COMPOSITE CONSTRUCTION FOR
HOME AND NORTH EUROPEAN MARKET.

MODEL J/C

### HERBERT LOMAS LIMITED, HANDFORTH, WILMSLOW, CHESHIRE
Telephone: WILMSLOW 5258 (5 Lines)   Telegrams: AMBULANCE, HANDFORTH
ALSO AT CHELTENHAM

---

*Herbert Lomas got in on the act a little later than Pilcher's, and again offered a range of ambulance bodies to suit different budgets.*

115

Some types of terrain were too difficult even for a Land Rover, and for those there were specialist conversions. The Cuthbertson conversion replaced the wheels by track units, and added power-assisted steering to give reasonable control. The Roadless conversion used truck axles and tractor tyres. Both were very expensive, and both remained quite rare.

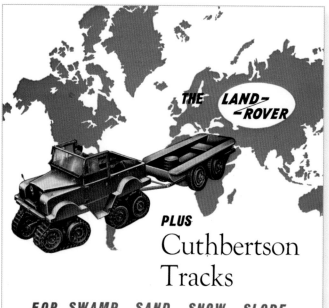

THE **LAND ROVER**

PLUS

# Cuthbertson Tracks

### FOR SWAMP, SAND, SNOW, SLOPE

**James A. Cuthbertson Limited,**
**Station Road, BIGGAR,**
**Lanarkshire ML12 6DQ, U.K.**
Telephone: 0899-20020
Telex: 7779
Telegrams: "Mechadrain Biggar"

Directors:
JAMES A. CUTHBERTSON O.B.E., M.I.AGR.E.
COLIN MacGREGOR B.L., N.P.
ARCHIBALD McM. MILLAR    ANDREW H. WILSON
ROBERT WALKINSHAW    JOHN ROBERTSON
JAMES T. MORTON

The simple robust construction without any special transmission parts and the articulated power assisted steering give reliability and ease of control.
Supplied as a conversion kit or complete, the unit is easily re-converted to a normal wheeled Land Rover.
The normal Land Rover suspension coupled with the special oscillating undercarriage gives excellent stability and a smooth ride over the roughest country.
Supplied as standard with general purpose track grousers the unit has good hard road and off the road performance.
Special grousers can be provided for special conditions if the vehicle has not to use the public road.
Mud wings for road work can be provided, also hydraulic winches and most of the standard Land Rover accessories.
Special 10 cwt. trailers are available using the redundant Land Rover wheels.

---

# THE ROADLESS 109

Designed and developed with the assistance of The Rover Co. Ltd.
(Technical Sales Department)

Tested for over two years and thousands of miles, under a variety of severe conditions, including forestry, bogs, cross country and good and bad road surfaces. Large diameter wheels ensure low rolling resistance and high ground clearance on extreme surface conditions.

High drawbar pull . . . Wide wheel base gives excellent stability on side slopes . . . Heavy duty suspension built for cross country work . . . Will wade through water up to 2 ft. 6 ins. deep . . . Large diameter and wide tyre section gives low ground pressure necessary for bog and soft sand.

**ROADLESS TRACTION LIMITED**
HOUNSLOW · MIDDLESEX · ENGLAND
*Telephone: Hounslow 6421*

---

There was a refuse wagon conversion from Eagle, while Precision Engineering offered a conveyor, which was taken up by some airline operators as a baggage loader.

## SPECIFICATION & DETAILS

**3 CUB. YDS. REFUSE COLLECTION BODY**

**DETAILS**
Body : 6' 0" long x 5' 0" wide x 1' 7½" deep.
4 sliding covers, 1' 9" camber.
Overall dimensions : 15' 3" long.
5' 4" wide, 6' 2" high.
45° angle of tip.
Loading line 4' 4" U.L.
Unladen Weight 35 Cwts.

**SPECIFICATION**
Body constructed of steel sheets, all joints electrically welded, and built on a sturdy steel sub-frame. The sides have radius corners for clean discharge and the wheel arches are gently radiused.
A heavy rubber bumper bar is fitted along top of sides to prevent bin damage and is easily replaceable.
Taildoor is top hinged and secured by cam type locking bar. Covers are "Easi-Slide" clip type in two sections each side. Tipping gear is hand operated telescopic screw type and has two winding handles.
Mudwings are fitted over rear wheels.
Finish : painted in standard Land Rover Grey.

**OPTIONAL EXTRAS**
Taildoor can be fitted with a rubber seal and made watertight. Vehicle can be finish painted to customer's own requirements at extra cost.

Order chassis cab specification under No. S2006 109' Diesel. or No. S2005 109' Petrol.

**LAND ROVER EXTRAS REQUIRED—**
SPARE WHEEL CARRIER ON BONNET HEAVY DUTY SUSPENSION

Printed by A. Tomes Ltd., 46, Bedford Street, Leamington Spa.

---

# MOY

## CONVEYORS

**ALL-HYDRAULIC MOUNTED**
**LAND-ROVER CONVERSION**
APPROVED BY THE ROVER COMPANY LTD.

**LAND ROVER**

These Conveyors have been designed to meet the ever-increasing demand for reduction in time and manual effort in the loading and unloading of packaged goods or loose (bulk) materials in applications where mobility of the equipment is of primary importance. They are available in two models, Standard and Low-Level.

**THE STANDARD CONVEYOR,** mounted on the 109" wheelbase LAND-ROVER Truck, can be supplied fitted either with an endless belt suitable for packaged goods only, or with one suitable for loose materials or small packages. The equipment can be quickly dismounted from the LAND-ROVER, thus freeing the vehicle for other duties.

**THE LOW-LEVEL CONVEYOR,** which has been designed specifically as an **AIRCRAFT LOADER,*** is mounted on the 88" wheelbase Regular LAND-ROVER with modified bodywork and offset steering. It is fitted with an endless belt suitable for packaged goods only. The low overall height and exceptionally low discharge or feed-on heights available at both ends make it particularly suitable for under-belly work with aircraft, and for gaining access to low or awkwardly situated freight compartments to which access by larger vehicles would be impossible.
* Code Name: SPALE (Self-Propelled Aircraft Loading Equipment).

TODAY'S PRICE AND FURTHER PARTICULARS AVAILABLE ON REQUEST FROM:—

**PRECISION ENGINEERING PRODUCTS (SUFFOLK) LTD.,**
**BURY ST. EDMUNDS,    ENGLAND.    Tel. 2603**

## Cuthbertson Snowplough

**LAND-ROVER**

# FARMERS! ESTATES! COUNCILS!

Fit the new Cuthbertson snowplough to your Land Rover for a really *high speed* snow clearance.
Made by Scotland's largest snowplough manufacturers the makers of the famous "Hi-lift" snowplough. This machine is backed by snow clearance experience second to none.
A specially designed "V" type blade ensures ploughing stability through drifted snow, at speed of 25 m.p.h., and throws the snow well clear of the roadway.

## J. A. CUTHBERTSON LTD

BIGGAR SCOTLAND    Telephone: BIGGAR 20    Telegrams: MECHADRAIN

---

LEAFLET No. 9a/3/69

## The Atkinson Bull-Angledozer and Snowplough (Howie System)

**LAND-ROVER**

## You can fit to your LAND-ROVER

for Builders : Contractors : Farmers : Municipalities

## Simple and quick to fit, operate or remove

no drilling or alterations to the vehicle

## Atkinson's of Clitheroe Limited

Kendal Street : Clitheroe : Lancashire

Telephone: Clitheroe 2211.
Telex: 63211
Cables: Spreaders Clitheroe

A MEMBER OF THE SOLAR INDUSTRIES GROUP

---

*The Land Rover was a "natural" as a snow-plough, and several conversions were made available in different countries. The three illustrated here were among the UK-market options. The Cuthbertson type was probably not introduced before 1963, but is nevertheless seen attached to a Series I Land Rover. Atkinson's bought out the Howie interests during the 1960s.*

---

## THE HOWIE BULL-ANGLEDOZER and SNOWPLOUGH

**LAND-ROVER**

## YOU can fit to YOUR LANDROVER

*for*

Builders

Contractors

Farmers

Municipalities

SIMPLE AND QUICK TO FIT, OPERATE OR REMOVE

No drilling or alterations to the vehicle.

## J. B. Howie Ltd. a subsidiary of
## Atkinson's of Clitheroe Limited

KENDAL STREET    CLITHEROE    LANCASHIRE
Telephone: Clitheroe 645 (5 lines)    Telex: 63211    Cables: Spreaders Clitheroe

A MEMBER OF THE SOLAR INDUSTRIES GROUP

---

# D-B

## ARTICULATED LAND-ROVER

**LAND-ROVER**

MODEL PD35FS 35 cwt. LOW LOADER      MODEL QD45FS 45 cwt. POLE CARRIER

- A versatile, lightweight articulated vehicle, equally at home on or off the road.

- Wide range of semi-trailer designs for every purpose.

- Detachable pick-up body for quick and simple attachment to Land-Rover when Trailer is not in use.

- Automatic fifth wheel coupling and all fittings supplied as kit for easy fitting to chassis and cab unit.

- Existing vehicles can be converted.

- Does not affect the fitting of the majority of Rover approved equipment.

MANUFACTURED BY

## B. DIXON-BATE LIMITED,
## CHESTER

ENGLAND

---

*Land Rover had actually made its own fifth-wheel conversion in the early 1950s, but it was a unique factory "special". For public consumption, the job was handed over to Dixon-Bate, the towing specialists.*

*More than one company catered for the very specialist mobile cinema market. Most such vehicles belonged to public health agencies in Africa, which would set up temporary cinemas in the villages. The vehicle had to be self-contained, carrying screen, loudspeakers and playing equipment, and providing its own power source as well.*

*Moving livestock by Land Rover was far less common in Britain than it was on the much larger farms of Australia and New Zealand. Nevertheless, there was a need, and PD Stevens & Sons stepped in to meet it.*

*Campers were a growing business in the later 1950s and the 1960s, and the best-known Land Rover conversion was by Martin Walter, who used the Dormobile brand name. The roof was made of GRP and was hinged, to give a low profile for travelling and standing room inside when stationary.*

*Land Rovers could also be turned into mobile compressors, and this example was by Atlas Copco.*

Breakdown trucks on the Land Rover were also quite popular with small independent garages. This was the Harvey Frost offering, which had been available since the 1950s.

Few Land Rover drivers were ever pampered by the Bostrom shock-absorbing seat – but there must have been enough interest for the company to produce this special sales leaflet.

For vehicles that were regularly heavily laden, Aeon offered these rubber spring assisters. Many were used on vehicles converted for special duties, as the picture of the fire tender suggests.

Freewheeling front hubs were originally intended to reduce the drag of the drive components to the front axle. Wear on those components was also reduced, and so was noise, but an additional advantage was a slight improvement in fuel economy. Land Rover would seize on this during the 1970s, when fuel consumption suddenly became a major concern.

# A MILITARY SPECIAL

*An artist's illustrations did the job effectively for the first Lightweight sales catalogue in 1971, showing the vehicles as they were by that stage with headlamps on the front wings. In the background, soldiers remove the demountable elements of the body and prepare vehicles for heliporting, and one vehicle is shown being carried underneath a typical military helicopter of the time. The official name was always the Half-Ton Land Rover, although few people ever called it that.*

During the 1960s, the Land Rover engineers were prepared to bend over backwards to satisfy military requirements, especially if those requirements came from the British armed forces. Military orders were usually for sizeable fleets, and it was always worth Solihull taking the extra trouble to gain big orders.

So when the Royal Marines needed vehicles light enough to be carried ashore by helicopter from their commando carriers, Land Rover scrambled to shed weight from the standard 88-inch model of the time. It was difficult, and in the end was only achieved by redesigning the body, fitting narrower axles (to suit transport aircraft with narrow fuselages) and making certain non-essential items demountable so that they could be left behind for heliporting. Ironically, by the time the Military Half-Ton (which has always been known by its familiar name of Lightweight) entered production in 1968, the latest heavy-lift helicopters were capable of carrying a standard 88-inch Land Rover.

*These two pictures (above and above right) show a version of the Lightweight that was never put into production, although a prototype certainly existed and the artist must have seen it. Both the mobile radio station and the LHD vehicle have a "pram hood" design, with what was in effect a folding convertible top. All production models with canvas roofs in fact had the standard demountable style of canvas tilt. The mobile radio station would have had a military-standard 24-volt electrical system.*

Nevertheless, the exercise was certainly not wasted. The Army liked the look of these stripped-out machines, and decided to order them in quantity. The Lightweight very soon took over from the standard Series IIA as the standard military short-wheelbase model. Series IIA Lightweights continued in production until 1972, some months after civilian production had switched to Series III types, in order to meet large orders. From 1970, they had been modified slightly; the original models had headlamps in the grille panel, but new lighting regulations in some European countries where the British Army operated as part of NATO forces obliged Land Rover to move the headlamps to the wing fronts.

By 1971, Solihull was prepared to offer these special military models to other military authorities, and so the first sales catalogues were produced. The Lightweight continued right through the Series III era, updated in detail with elements of the new Series III specification.

Instruments and auxiliary controls are grouped centrally and include water temperature and oil temperature gauges. Dual windscreen wipers are driven by a single concealed motor and carry washer equipment, operated by a central push-button.

The vehicle illustrated opposite, is built to 24-volt FFR specification and has two 12-volt batteries installed between the front seats. On 12-volt models, this space is normally occupied by a second passenger seat.

Some things never change, and the general appearance of the Lightweight didn't, at least after the headlamps had moved out to the wings. By 1982, when this catalogue was issued, ordinary photographs were in vogue for promotional material. At top right is one of the "tank-buster" models, with 106mm gun.

A helicopter features in the background of this picture as well, but its task was not to carry the Land Rover. This is a casevac situation, with wounded soldiers being brought to the helicopter by a Lightweight equipped as an improvised stretcher carrier.

The Lightweight is seen here in semi-stripped down form, as a mobile weapons carrier. In practice, such a model did emerge early in the Series III period after an order from Saudi Arabia; the weapon fitted was a US-made 106mm recoilless rifle intended for anti-tank duties, and the conversion was carried out by specialists Marshall's of Cambridge. A few other overseas forces took examples, too.

# SERIES III

As always, Land Rover development was a continuous process, so when British Leyland management
suggested that it might be time for a change after
ten years of Series IIAs, there were already some ideas in
the pipeline. That change could not be very profound,
though. Solihull had already been granted a large chunk of
corporate money to get its new Range Rover into production in 1970, and there were more pressing demands for
investment elsewhere.

The result was really an upgraded Series IIA, although it
was given additional status and sales appeal by being called a
Series III. The model mix was exactly as it had been for the
last of the Series IIAs, and the engines were unchanged.
Nevertheless, there were some worthwhile suspension and
gearbox improvements (synchromesh on all forward gears
was a definite advance, even if it had been pioneered on the
last Series IIA Station Wagons) a much-improved dashboard
(developed mainly to meet overseas regulations about occu-

pant protection in a collision), and a built-in heater (though
even this was not standard for hot-climate markets). You
could recognise a Series III by its new ABS plastic radiator
grille and by the flat hinges for the side doors, which had
been developed to reduce external protrusions for those
markets that worried about such things.

The Series III was the last of the leaf-sprung Land Rovers,
but it would go on to become the type with the longest
production life. The very last Series III was built in mid-1985
– 14 years after the type's autumn 1971 introduction. The
Series I models had been in production for just 10 years; the
Series IIs for only three years; and the Series IIAs for 10 years.

## GEARBOX

There is now synchromesh engagement for all forward gears thus
eliminating the need for special gear-
changing technique in respect of first
and second. These speeds now have
constant mesh helical gears in place
of the spur-tooth dog engagement
gears previously used. They give considerably quieter operation and improved life. Additionally, the strength
of reverse gear has been significantly
increased by widening the tooth contact area, and a new oil sealing
arrangement is fitted between the
gearbox front cover and the clutch
housing.

## CLUTCH

All models now have a 9½ in. (241
mm.) diaphragm spring clutch—previously only fitted to diesel and six-
cylinder models. This not only gives
improved reliability and life but the
spring mechanism provides for lighter
operational pressures.

*It didn't look much, and there was no
reason why it should, but the Series III
gearbox now had synchromesh on all
forward gears. It also came with a new
gear lever, featuring a ball-shaped
grip instead of the flat-topped type
of the Series IIA. As this page
from the advance information
leaflet notes, there was now
a larger-diameter clutch
(actually the earlier
heavy-duty type).*

## MORE STRENGTH

A larger, high-capacity rubber sleeved bush is used for the chassis location of the front spring shackle on 109-in. wheelbase models. Also, extra reinforcing plates are welded under and inside the chassis frame to give greater support below the rear mounting of the front spring, enabling the vehicle to withstand unusually severe ditching.

## SMOOTHER HINGES

Exterior body projections have been considerably reduced by the fitting of restyled windscreen, bonnet and door hinges. A smoother, safer line has thus been achieved.

## AXLES

All 109-in. wheelbase Land-Rovers are now fitted with a rear axle of increased capacity, both structurally and as a drive unit. It is equivalent to the axle previously offered at extra cost for continuous heavy duty operations. The half-shafts are some 30 per cent. stronger than those currently fitted. An improved material is introduced for stub axles and swivel bearing housings on 109-in. wheelbase models.

*No reason to get excited, as Bob Dylan had written a few years earlier in the song, All along the Watchtower. The changes for the Series III really were evolutionary, with reinforced suspension, new door hinges and a stronger rear axle on 109 models.*

## MORE SAFETY & REFINEMENT— GREATER STRENGTH & RELIABILITY

The basic design of the Land-Rover has remained virtually unchanged during the twenty-three years this ubiquitous vehicle has been in existence. Nevertheless, today's Land-Rovers are very different from the first models that were produced, having undergone a process of progressive development to fit them for the ever-increasing demands made upon them by operators throughout the world.
Further developments are shortly to be announced in a Series III version of the Land-Rover. Their object is to provide greater safety and refinement and an even higher degree of strength and reliability.

Most of the changes apply to chassis components and do not affect the appearance of the vehicle, but two major visual changes are a redesigned front grille which afford an easy means of recognising the latest models, and a new facia and instrument layout.
We believe that the improvements detailed in this leaflet will be a valuable contribution to the continuing good name of the Land-Rover, and give even greater force to the title 'The World's Most Versatile Vehicle'.

*This picture of a Series III had been only mildly airbrushed, mainly around the tyres. The new grille was just enough to make the difference, and of course the Land Rover was still primarily a commercial vehicle; in the commercial market, buyers did not expect visual interest or regular changes of appearance.*

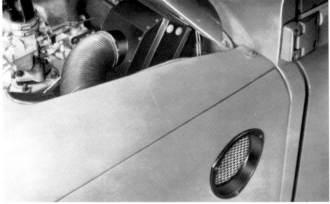

## CONTROLS

The driving compartment shows several important changes which bring it more into line with modern car practice and give an added air of refinement. The two circular instruments are now recessed into a binnacle in front of the driver together with ancillary controls and warning lights for oil pressure, headlamp main beam and cold start. Switches have also been moved and are placed within comfortable reach of a driver wearing properly-adjusted safety harness. A combined direction indicator, horn, headlamp flasher and dip switch control stalk is steering-column mounted.

## HEATING

A more powerful, fresh air heater with an output equivalent to 4½ Kw and available as a factory-fitted optional extra, replaces the previous type.

## OTHER FEATURES

Servo-assisted brakes are standard on all six-cylinder models and four-cylinder Station Wagons, and are available as a factory-fitted optional extra on other four-cylinder 109-in. wheelbase models. New brake drums with better heat-dissipating qualities give improved anti-fade performance. Translucent brake fluid reservoir for easy checking of fluid level.

Brake pipe layout simplified for easier inspection.
Alternator replaces the dynamo as standard equipment on all models, with battery located in engine compartment. Hazard warning system available as factory-fitted optional extra.
Combined steering-column lock and ignition switch fitted where legally required.

## FACIA

Padded crash rails run the full width of the vehicle above and below the facia parcel shelf. Incorporated in the upper rail are face-level fresh air vents with built-in fly screens, and heater outlets for windscreen demisting. The lower portion offers protection for the knees and has provision for three auxiliary instruments as well as a radio and loudspeaker installation. Outlet vents for the fresh-air heater are also included.

*The new dashboard was quite different from what had gone before. For a start, it set the instruments in front of the driver rather than in the middle of the vehicle. It was also made of plastic rather than metal, and those sliding controls on the outboard edge were for the new heater. The heater came with its own air intake that was let into the wing and, as the heater box was always on the opposite side to the steering wheel, so was the air intake.*

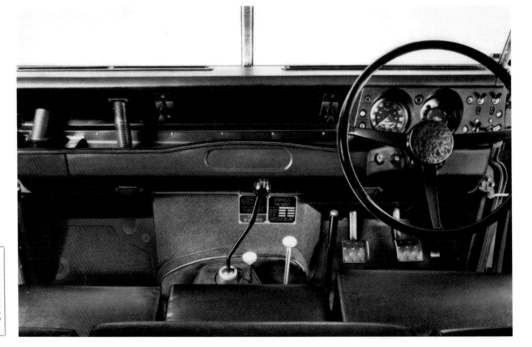

**AXLES**
Front and rear axles are fully-floating and have spiral bevel drive.

**CHASSIS FRAME**
Welded steel box-section of great strength. Six cross-members give torsional and diagonal rigidity.

**BRAKES**
Hydraulic. Handbrake operates transmission brake behind transfer box.

**SUSPENSION**
Underslung semi-elliptic springs controlled by double-acting hydraulic telescopic shock absorbers.

**ENGINES**
Choice of two units: four-cylinder, 2¼-litre petrol or four-cylinder, 2¼-litre diesel.

**POWER TAKE-OFF**
Provision for centre and rear power take-off drives. Hydraulic or capstan winch may be fitted at front.

**BODY**
Steel fittings, including bulkhead and front grille surround, are either treated and painted or heavily galvanised. All body panels are of non-corrodible light alloy.

*Photography was now beginning to dominate in sales catalogues, and for the first time there was a photograph of a chassis rather than a coloured illustration. It worked well enough, too, showing all the main features of an 88-inch petrol model.*

Land-Rover 88in. Wheelbase Regular

*Yet there was still a laziness, or a lack of budget, associated with Land Rover catalogues. The cover image of the September 1971 Series III catalogue was the one that had been used for the late Series IIA models (see page 109), with the new grille airbrushed in. Inside, Series IIA DXC 203G had been modified to show the latest K registration and sport the new grille as well.*

125

The Range Rover was introduced in 1970, a year before the Series III. Even though Rover had insisted that early examples carried a rear decal reading "by Land Rover", the car was usually marketed alone or alongside Rover saloons, and almost never alongside Land Rovers. An exception was made in the Netherlands, however. These two sales leaflets date from around 1980, and show Series III and Range Rover together. The lower inscription translates as "The new freedom", and suggests that advertising for the Series III Station Wagons, at least, was leaning towards leisure users.

"De nieuwe vrijheid."

By 1974, a budget had been found for some decent photography, and this picture showed the Series III seats. They were based on the earlier De Luxe seats, and were pictured in the more luxurious surroundings of a 109 Station Wagon with its standard floor trim and door cards. It was a six-cylinder model, too, as the straight gear lever seen here makes clear.

# SEVENTIES SPECIALS

The Special Projects Department continued to examine and test new conversions by specialist companies, although by the time of the Series IIIs a large number of popular conversions had already been granted Land Rover Approval. Land Rovers still had an appeal to those who worked on the land, and there were several conversions intended for that market. The emergency services were still taking quantities of fire tenders and ambulances – and Land Rovers also had an appeal to Police forces for some duties, although these vehicles tended to have a near-standard specification. There were dedicated "leisure" conversions, too.

Political upheavals in the Middle East also had their effect on Land Rovers. As the price of crude oil shot up in 1973-1974, and fuel consumption became an issue for drivers of all types of vehicle, Solihull had to do something to reduce the Land Rover's thirst. The solution came in the form of a bolt-on overdrive that was manufactured by Fairey – otherwise makers of winches – and could be fitted to any Land Rover, new or old.

*In June 1972, Land Rover issued a booklet listing the approved conversions and equipment available for the Series III. The title was not its best feature, although the pictures on the cover gave a clear idea of the contents. Even though colour photography had more or less taken over for the main sales catalogues, a decision was made to use drawings for this one.*

*Quite rare but nonetheless very useful for carrying livestock was this stake-side conversion. It was made by PD Stevens.*

*Crop-spraying conversions had been available for many years, and needed no modification to suit the Series III models. The booms folded up for travelling on the road.*

*There was more than one supplier of light recovery vehicles, which were built on the 109-inch chassis because this gave greater stability for towing than the 88.*

*For municipal authorities with only a small area to cover, a 109-based refuse carrier was a viable proposition. Introduced in the early 1960s, it was made by Eagle.*

Mobile welders had been around since the very earliest days of the Land Rover. The welding unit could be powered either from the centre PTO or the rear PTO. The drawing showing a rear PTO in use was taken directly from a much earlier photograph that showed the welding unit mounted to a 1958 Series II 109.

Fire appliance conversions were still available from several companies. Most were based on the 109 chassis, like the one illustrated, but there were conversions for the 88 as well. The formula usually included a first-aid water or foam tank, a fire pump, a small-diameter hose reel, a ladder and equipment lockers.

The armoured car built by Short Brothers in Belfast depended on the One Ton version of the 109 chassis. The design had been introduced in 1965 and had gradually been modified in line with customer requirements and with changes to the Land Rover itself. Most customers were outside the UK, although a few were used for a time in Northern Ireland.

The "cherry-picker" was another conversion that proved of value to some local authorities.

The Land Rover was recognised as an ideal expedition vehicle, but there were versions to suit those who simply enjoyed camping as well. Illlustrated here is a "sleeper" conversion on the 88-inch chassis, which provided enough accommodation for one person. The other picture shows the famous Dormobile conversion by Martin Walter, with its elevating roof. As many as four people could sleep in this 109-based model, although the top two bunks were best suited to young children.

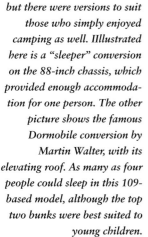

There is a tremendous range of specialised equipment available for use with the Land-Rover. A small selection is illustrated here, but any Land-Rover Distributor or Dealer will supply prices and details on request. Only equipment approved by Leyland Cars should be used otherwise the manufacturers warranty could be invalidated.

All Land-Rover Special Equipment has been tested to high levels of durability and quality to give years of trouble-free operation. All components can be fitted by your dealer or supplied in kit form with easy to follow, step-by-step fitting instructions. Competitively priced, these quality parts can enable you to undertake a greater variety of work with your Land-Rover.

▲ **Front winches.** A drum winch with a pull of 2270 kg. (5000 lb.) can be installed, with hydraulic or mechanical power to suit a variety of applications. Controllable from the cab or the front of the vehicle. A mechanically driven capstan winch, controlled from the front of the vehicle, is also available.

◄ **Lamp guards.** Rugged all metal construction to minimise lens damage and improve safety. Available for front and rear lights.

**Spare wheel carrier.** ▶ For mounting spare wheel on bonnet, increasing payload area. Provision for lock (not supplied).

◄ **Winch Accessories.** A selection of cables, polypropylene rope, hook shackle and pulley block are available to complete the winch operator's requirements.

**Jerry cans and brackets.** 20 litre (4.5 gallon) containers for storing extra fuel, or water, with easily fitted brackets. ▶

◄ **Undershield.** Gives full-width protection to front underside of vehicle. For exceptionally rough cross-country work.

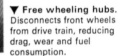

◄ **Rubber helper springs.** Maintain light-load handling characteristics by reducing spring deflection under load. (DO NOT increase payload capacity.)

▼ **Free wheeling hubs.** Disconnects front wheels from drive train, reducing drag, wear and fuel consumption.

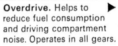

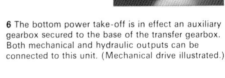

▲ **Centre and rear power take-off units.** As illustrated on the previous page, the power take-off units can be employed in a variety of ways. The rear power take-off can be fitted with a protective shield and cover, as shown above.

**Overdrive.** Helps to reduce fuel consumption and driving compartment noise. Operates in all gears. ▶

6 The bottom power take-off is in effect an auxiliary gearbox secured to the base of the transfer gearbox. Both mechanical and hydraulic outputs can be connected to this unit. (Mechanical drive illustrated.)

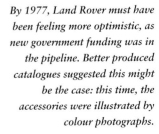

*The Fairey Overdrive was a rapid response to an urgent problem, and it could indeed reduce fuel consumption. How much depended on the driver's style and the type of driving. Fitting one wasn't all gain, however. It added yet another gear lever to the small forest in the cab, plus an additional selection of clunks and bangs down the driveline unless gears were changed with some sensitivity.*

*By 1977, Land Rover must have been feeling more optimistic, as new government funding was in the pipeline. Better produced catalogues suggested this might be the case: this time, the accessories were illustrated by colour photographs.*

# Land-Rover Special Conversions

The cross-country performance capabilities of the Land-Rover, its load carrying capacity and availability in chassis form all contribute to the demand for this vehicle as the basis for special conversions and for the fitting of specialist appliances. We show just a few examples here but full details of all approved equipment is available from any Land-Rover Distributor or Dealer. Left. Police, Fire and Ambulance service vehicles. Above. A cattle truck. A crop or verge sprayer. Right. A self-contained safari-type motor caravan. A snow-blade. A mobile crane.

*Some of the special conversions had also been photographed for the 1977 sales catalogue. In the fire engine picture on the left, the vehicle further from the camera is a forward-control Carmichael FT/6 conversion, pictured in Series IIA form on page 114. At top right is the Carawagon camper conversion of a 109 hardtop, with its distinctive pop-up roof.*

# THE LEYLAND PERIOD

Even though Land Rover had become part of British Leyland in 1967, you would hardly have noticed. BL left the Land Rover marque well alone for several years. There were other areas of the company that needed more urgent attention because they were losing money; the Land Rover business was continuing to make profits. So when the Series III models were launched in 1971, the latest corporate logo with its "flying wheel" and the British Leyland name alongside the Rover one was relegated firmly to the back of sales catalogues. A Land Rover was still a Land Rover.

Things began to change in 1974. The new Land Rover sales catalogues issued in March that year had the British Leyland logo on their covers, though it was relatively discreet. By 1976, the latest Leyland logo, with an L in the centre of the flying wheel, was starting to crop up all over the place, and by 1977 the Leyland name was often more prominent in sales literature than the Land Rover name.

These were uncomfortable years for the Land Rover marque in more ways than one, and they did not last. When British Leyland had run out of money at the end of 1974 and had gone crying to the government for help, the government stumped up the necessary to keep the company afloat in the short term, but immediately commissioned an investigation into the state of the company. Although there was a determined assault from many quarters on the recommendations of the Ryder Report when it was published in 1975, its recommendation that the Land Rover business should be separated from the rest of the car business did survive. In 1978, Land Rover Ltd was established as a standalone business unit within the Leyland empire, and was granted the first £30 million of a planned government support package. The Leyland days were over.

THE ROVER TRIUMPH RANGE

*Land Rover never did fit very well within the Rover-Triumph cars division that was established after the two companies lost their independent management in 1971. This is a July 1975 sales brochure that promotes the whole range of cars from both marques. And yet, despite the glamour of the Triumph sports cars and the prestige of the Rover saloons, it's a Land Rover that has been chosen for the cover.*

Land-Rover 88" Wheelbase Regular

*March 1974, and the British Leyland symbol appears for the first time on the front cover of a UK sales catalogue. It's discreet, but it's also unmissable. The Series IIIs advertised for sale have barely changed since 1971, and the shape of a Land Rover is so familiar that it is shown only in profile.*

131

# ![Leyland logo] Leyland International

**Land-Rover**

**Land Rover 106mm gun vehicle**

The "flying wheel" logo underwent a subtle change after 1975. The British Leyland words that had flanked it disappeared. Here it is prominently displayed on the cover of a military sales catalogue issued by Leyland International in 1976. Leyland International was supposed to look after all the group's overseas affairs, but wouldn't be associated with Land Rover for long. The sales catalogue was for a tank-buster derivative of the Series III Lightweight, mounting the US-made 106mm recoilless rifle. Originally developed for the Saudi Arabian armed forces in conjunction with Marshall's of Cambridge, the model was marketed globally from 1976.

The reproduction of colour photographs in print was improving, and Rover-British Leyland UK (as they were now called) made good use of the medium in sales literature. Although these shots were posed a little self-consciously for a June 1974 catalogue, they did show the Leyland-era Series III as it really looked.

**Leyland Savers**

**LAND-ROVER Overdrive Unit**

Your Land-Rover has a reputation to live up to. You bought it because it is capable of doing a specific job for you based on that reputation. Now Leyland offers you the opportunity to get even more out of your Land-Rover. Would you like to:

★ Increase road speed by up to 27·8% at the same engine speed?
★ Decrease petrol consumption by up to 16%?
★ Reduce engine and drive line wear?
★ Obtain greater flexibility—16 forward gear ratios?
★ Lengthen tyre life?
★ Reduce noise and driver fatigue?
★ Have full Leyland Cars backing?

How?
By fitting the Leyland Land-Rover overdrive unit. This precision built, fully synchromeshed, mechanically selected unit has no hydraulic or electrical connections, and is easily fitted in under 3 hours to all current Land-Rovers.
Your Dealer has full details.

BROWNCHURCH(Land-Rovers)LTD,
308-310 HARE ROW, off Cambridge Heath Rd,
LONDON, E.2
TEL: 01-729 3606 (2 LINES)
TELEX NO: 299397

*The "flying wheel" logo seemed to get everywhere. A close look at the number-plates of these three Series III models on the cover of a 1977 sales brochure shows it alongside the Land Rover name.*

*... and here it is again, this time inside the sales catalogue. Even the registration number of the vehicle is a sign of the times. Instead of being registered by Land Rover with their local Solihull authority, it had been registered in Birmingham by a centralised office within the Leyland organisation.*

**Land·Rover**

Today's Land-Rovers are stronger, safer and more reliable than ever before. There is a choice of Short or Long chassis versions, petrol or diesel power, a range of different body styles, optional equipment and a comprehensive selection of Leyland approved special appliances and bodies by specialist manufacturers.
For year-in, year-out operation in all types of terrain, in adverse weathers and climates, the four-wheel drive Land-Rover is still 'The World's Most Versatile Vehicle'.

**Leyland Savers**

**LAND-ROVER Free Wheeling Hubs**

Your Land-Rover is an ideal cross-country vehicle. Leyland now offer considerable savings for the Land-Rover man who spends only part of his time off the beaten track. Would you like to:

★ Reduce fuel consumption by up to 10%?
★ Reduce mechanical wear?
★ Reduce drive line drag?
★ Increase acceleration?
★ Lengthen tyre life?
★ Lighten steering?
★ Have easy disengagement of drive line?
★ Have full Leyland Cars backing?

How?
By fitting free wheeling hubs. Fitted in under half an hour. These components disengage the drive line from the front wheels with the simple turning of the clearly marked selector on the hub.
Your Dealer has full details.

BROWNCHURCH(Land-Rovers)LTD.
308-310 HARE ROW, off Cambridge Heath Rd,
LONDON, E.2
TEL: 01-729 3606 (2 LINES)
TELEX NO: 299397

*Once upon a time, the Land Rover Overdrive unit had been an approved accessory made by Fairey Winches of Tavistock. By 1978, it had become a Leyland Saver. The Fairey freewheeling front hubs had gone the same way. Meanwhile, the Unipart organisation became involved with Land Rover parts, and for a time spares came in boxes of corporate Leyland blue instead of the old yellow type with red Land Rover logos.*

The sign of quality LAND-ROVER GENUINE PARTS

*These pictures are of Station Wagon chassis, and come from a 1974 catalogue devoted to those models. The chassis in the foreground shows clearly how the 109 Station Wagon had its fuel tank mounted at the rear rather than under the seat. This arrangement had been in place since the start of Series II production; the six-cylinder 109s had also had a rear-mounted tank from the beginning, although that was differently shaped to make room for the propshaft needed if the rear PTO option was fitted.*

**BODY**
Steel fittings, including bulkhead and front grille surround, are either treated and painted or heavily galvanised.

**TYRES**
A large range of alternative and special purpose tyres (examples illustrated) is available to equip the Land-Rover for the prevailing conditions.

### LAND ROVER 88 DIESEL
Ormai da 30 anni, esploratori, tecnici, imprese di costruzione, forze di polizia e militari e moltissimi privati utilizzano la LAND ROVER perché non esistono altri veicoli dotati delle sue particolari caratteristiche. La LAND ROVER, robusta, sicura e utilissima dovunque. Potrete trovarla nei luoghi più impensati dove nessun altra automobile puó arrivare. Essa rappresenta una riuscita sintesi di soluzioni tecniche ormai collaudate attraverso lunghi anni di esperienze. Di essa esistono versioni sia con il motore a benzina che diesel e molte versioni dotate dei più diversi equipaggiamenti. La LAND ROVER con le sue 4 ruote motrici può operare su qualsiasi tipo di terreno ed è certamente il più versatile dei veicoli.

*The Leyland days may have been over in the UK after 1978, but the name lingered in some overseas markets where the ins and outs of the British motor industry were less well understood. This Italian sales leaflet dates from 1981, and the vehicle shows the wing repeater lamps that were required in that country. The Italian diesel 88 Station Wagon also came with overdrive as standard.*

# THE 101 ONE-TONNE

**101" FORWARD CONTROL MILITARY LAND ROVER**

By the mid-1960s, the British Army was planning a new generation of field artillery which would be larger and, inevitably, heavier than previous types. The artillery regiments were used to towing their guns with Land Rovers, but it began to look as if the new 155mm howitzer that would enter service some time in the next decade would be too heavy for a standard model.

As soon as they heard about this, Land Rover set to work to build a vehicle that would be able to cope. Their first attempt was essentially a bigger Land Rover, with a 3-litre six-cylinder engine, but it ended up very different from the standard models and the military was not very impressed. The MoD then came up with a more detailed specification for the artillery tractor it wanted. More or less handed the contract on a plate, Land Rover got on with designing and developing the vehicle. To meet the military requirement, it would be a forward-control model with maximum cargo space within a minimum footprint, and it would have to have Rover's most powerful engine.

Early prototypes had the 3-litre engine, but then the new alloy 3.5-litre V8 became available and improved the vehicle enormously. Some work was done on powered-trailer systems, in which a power take-off in the tow hitch drove a propshaft to the axle of the trailer or – in this case – the gun. In the end, the 155mm howitzer was built without its powered gun carriage, not least because these systems had given trouble in trials. However, the new Land Rover did go into production, with a wheelbase of 101 inches and a military load rating of a metric tonne, from which came its alternative name of One Tonne.

Production lasted from 1974 to 1978, and almost all those built went to the British armed forces. A few were sold to overseas military authorities. Most were General Service types with a full-length canvas tilt, but there were also ambulances and hard-body vehicles used mostly for communications and other electronics duties. Rover did have hopes of developing a civilian-market version to replace the old Series IIB Forward Control, but close adherence to the military requirement had left them with a vehicle that needed major work to pass the Construction and Use regulations that applied to civilian commercial vehicles. Likely sales volumes did not justify the expected expense. Nevertheless, the design did have a new lease of life when it was passed to Santana in Spain and redeveloped as their 2000 Forward Control.

*Land Rover began looking for additional customers as soon as the British military contract had been agreed, and the sales catalogue for the 101 was issued in November 1974. By that stage, only the prototypes had been photographed in action, and most of those looked very different from the production models. So a local artist called Pittaway was called in to produce some drawings – and the results were quite stunning. This was the cover of the catalogue, showing a 101 in its role as gun tractor.*

Airportability was one of the military requirements, and Land Rover was well aware of the weight limitations associated with helicopters after its experience with the Lightweight. So the 101 was designed with demountable body elements so that weight could be reduced if necessary. The example slung underneath this helicopter has been stripped to its essentials for the trip.

The 101 is shown here towing a military trailer. The side view is of one equipped with a powered axle; the special trailer hitch and propshaft to the trailer axle's differential are visible. The registration number suggests that the illustrations may have been drawn as early as 1972, even though the catalogue was issued in 1974.

This was one of the potential applications that didn't come to fruition. It shows the 101 equipped as an airfield crash tender. The RAF did take 101s, but not for this role.

The artist had clearly spent some time observing trials or demonstrations with a 101 acting as gun tractor. The gun barrel would normally be carried across the trails of its carriage when the gun was being towed; the picture with the barrel in the firing position shows why. One of these vehicles carries the Nokken winch mounted below the body that was unique to the 101s but was not fitted to every example.

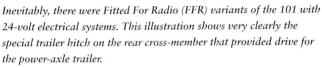

Inevitably, there were Fitted For Radio (FFR) variants of the 101 with 24-volt electrical systems. This illustration shows very clearly the special trailer hitch on the rear cross-member that provided drive for the power-axle trailer.

One of the prototypes had been trialled with Goodyear Terra-Tires, which were designed to spread the weight of the vehicle and give traction in boggy ground. It had been hitched to a powered-axle trailer, too. This was a demonstration not likely to be repeated (and in the end the Terra-Tire option was rejected), and so the artist based his drawing on a photograph taken at those trials.

The Terra-Tire vehicle figures in the background of this illustration, too. The 101 in the foreground shows the flat panelling and functional, almost brutal, appearance of the 101 in General Service trim.

The Royal Air Force (RAF Regiment) took a number of 101s as Rapier missile tractors. The Rapiers were surface-to-air missiles used for the defence of airfields, both temporary and permanent, and a crew is seen preparing the Rapier trailer here. The missiles were carried in boxes that can be seen stacked in the 101 with its back in view.

Pure invention! The artist was working blind here, because there were no examples of the 101 ambulance to study when he made his illustrations. The open back end of an ambulance is clearly based on a standard military 109 ambulance with Marshall bodywork, and the 101 on the right has a cutaway rear end (like the 109s, where it was necessary for the vehicles to negotiate the access ramps of landing craft). In reality, the 101 ambulance – also by Marshall's – would look rather different.

One of the 101 prototypes had been fitted experimentally with Beeswing missiles fired from a launcher in the load bed. The artist was clearly working from a photograph here, and that original photograph shows how different the front end of the early six-cylinder prototypes looked.

Another role envisaged for the 101 was as a portee for the lightweight anti-tank WOMBAT weapon. Such weapons were carried by ordinary 109-inch ("three-quarter-ton") British military Land Rovers, but the 101s had other roles to perform.

Here, the back of a 101 is pictured with unspecified electronic equipment, possibly for fire control. Some 101s were used for electronic warfare, but these had box-type bodies.

# SANTANA

Santana Series IIIs entered production in 1974 and were initially closely related to the Solihull types, but the Spanish company soon began to introduce new varieties. From 1976 it had six-cylinder petrol and diesel engines, derived from the existing Solihull four-cylinder types with the full agreement and assistance of the parent company. As these needed a longer engine bay, new front end designs began to arrive. From 1979, the Santana 2000 Forward Control had no UK-built equivalent, although it was actually a derivative of the military-only 101 One Tonne.

As the 1980s opened, Santana Land Rovers began to diverge even more from the parent product. A brightly-painted Ligero 88 was introduced, essentially a leisure-market derivative of Santana's military 88, itself distantly related to the Lightweight. Roof panels were moulded from GRP. There were no coil-sprung Santanas; instead, the Spanish company used parabolic leaf springs to improve ride comfort. Santana developed a five-speed gearbox, a turbocharged 2¼-litre engine in 1983, and switched to gear-driven camshafts in preference to Solihull's belt-driven design. A Series IIIA model was introduced, with no bulkhead ventilators but an air intake in the bonnet instead, and there was a 119-inch Gran Capacidad model on leaf springs instead of Solihull's 127-inch type on coils.

After the final Series III models had been built, Santana went their own way with Series IV types, still on leaf springs but sharing some front end similarities with Solihull's coil-sprung models. By 1990, the two companies and their products had grown too far apart for their relationship to continue, and it was formally severed.

*Many Santana-built Station Wagons were fitted with bright metal wheel embellishers like the ones on this example from the 1970s.*

## Model 109" 4 cylinders

Of greater carrying capacity than the short wheel base Land-Rover, the 109" Land-Rover still retains the same exceptional mobility and do-anything, go-anywhere characteristics.

Land-Rover 4 wheel drive Station Wagons are a familiar sight over the world. They are performing with distinction on major construction sites, on expeditions and safaris, at airports, in national and international organizations anywhere, in fact, where unrestricted transport of personnel and equipment is needed all the year round, in all climates, under all conditions.

Their greatest advantage over other forms of transport is their ability to overcome adverse terrain and reach normally inaccessible places.

HARD TOP

PICK-UP

CHASSIS

STATION WAGON

**BASICO**

**CABINA
TOLDO LONA 3/4**

**CABINA CHASIS**

**NORMAL**

**ESPECIAL**

**LAND ROVER SANTANA 109"**

**6 CILINDROS 3.429 c.c.**

With the arrival of longer six-cylinder engines came the first of Santana's own front-end designs. This was the first, introduced in 1976. The engine itself – pictured is the diesel version – was designed with Solihull's involvement. It shared the bore and stroke dimensions and the overall architecture of the 2¼-litre engine, and with six cylinders instead of four had a swept volume of 3429cc.

This is from an English-language Santana catalogue: the company exported to many countries where the Solihull product was not sold. Note that the hardtop model (Usually called the "Normal" in Spanish, as the fourth picture shows) was in fact a window hardtop. The truck cab 109 also normally had a window soft top.

**LAND ROVER SANTANA 2000**

**un "todo terreno" excepcional.**

The Santana 2000 was in fact the Spanish company's derivative of the 101 Forward Control. It always had six-cylinder engines and was built for both civilian and military users, but fewer than 1000 were made in total.

Even the owner's handbook was special for the Santana Series IIIs. It was not simply a translation into Spanish of the Solihull-produced item. One major difference was that Santana switched to metric dimensions long before Solihull did – and the parts it manufactured were made to those dimensions rather than Imperial ones.

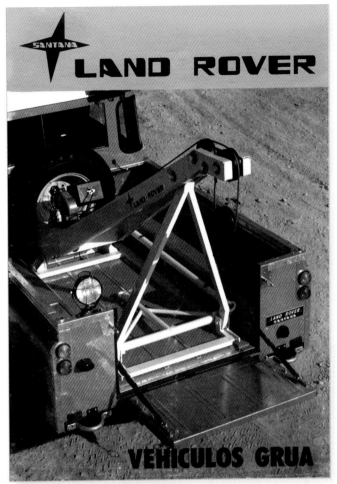

The Santana-built Series III Station Wagon was recognisably a Series III, but it had some major differences from the Solihull variety. Visible on this early 1980s model are the moulded GRP roof panel, the winding door windows and the relocated door handles, which were both at the same height. Even the wheels were painted a different colour – in this case silver, rather than to match the body.

Santana also made their own special-purpose conversions. There were three varieties of crane – mechanical, hydraulic and electric. This is the electric one, based on Warn winch components. Note the Land Rover Santana rear badge, used in the 1980s. The ambulance conversions were based on the "Normal" 109 or window hardtop model.

Va equipado con: techo de poliéster, ventanas alpinas y trampillas de aireación interior; parabrisas con cristal de una pieza (con tres brazos limpiaparabrisas incorporados); luneta térmica en ventanilla trasera con lava y limpiaparabrisas; doble depósito de combustible (con capacidad de 92 litros); paragolpes delantero y trasero, en poliéster, con estribo incorporado; rueda libre en el eje delantero y servo-freno, que le permite, bajo cualquier circunstancia y con el mínimo esfuerzo, su detención en el espacio de terreno requerido.

Su estudiado diseño interior ha permitido conseguir una capacidad de nueve plazas, manteniendo en todas ellas el máximo confort para los pasajeros.

En definitiva: en todos los elementos que lo componen se ha conseguido una perfecta combinación potencia / confort, que hace que su conducción sea un placer.

## LAND ROVER SANTANA CAZORLA,

Compruebe sus ventajas

The front-end design of the six-cylinder models went through further evolutions that were unique to Santana. This version dates from 1982, and was used on the Cazorla models, which were roughly equivalent to County Station Wagons. Even the front bumper was special.

There were no turbocharged Series IIIs from the factory at Solihull, and when Land Rover did introduce a turbocharged engine in 1986, it was for the coil-sprung models and was based on the 2.5-litre engine. Santana couldn't wait that long; they designed their own turbocharged derivative of the 2¼-litre engine and had it in Series IIIA models during 1984.

The Super was a model based on the Series IIIA, which was distinguished visually by an absence of bulkhead ventilation flaps. This is an 88 Super Turbo Station Wagon from 1984, with perforated disc wheels, a single-piece windscreen and a new grille broadly similar to that introduced on the coil-sprung One Ten in the UK. It also has the side stripes that Santana saw as essential for leisure-market customers. The doors have winding windows, and the vents in the wing panel are for the turbocharger air intake.

The characteristic ledge in the GRP roof is visible on this 88 Station Wagon which still has sliding Perspex windows in the front doors. It is also fitted with freewheeling front hubs of Spanish manufacture.

The Santana dashboard was already evolving its own way, too. The one pictured is from a 1984 Super model and was very different from the Solihull type.

The Cazorla continued to evolve. Here it is in Series IIIA guise, with the flush-front styling introduced in 1984. The front wheels have freewheeling hubs.

The Ligero was a bright, leisure-market derivative of Santana's 88 Militar, a military-special model related to Solihull's military Light-weight. It was an imaginative concept, and it worked. Spain had the climate for it, of course; such a model would have found few buyers in rainy Britain, and besides, the country was not yet ready for a dedicated leisure-market Land Rover.

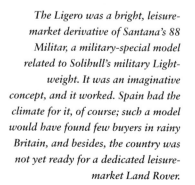

# NEW ENGINES

As far as the Land Rover was concerned, the outcome of the Ryder Report on the state of British Leyland was all good. The report recommended that Land Rover should be turned into a standalone business unit, and with that in mind the marque was separated from Rover-Triumph in 1978 and became a company called Land Rover Ltd with its own management. It was also granted a large sum of government investment capital. This was allocated in two stages – Stage 1 delivered £30 million in 1978, and Stage 2 would deliver a further £250 million in 1981.

Land Rover already knew exactly what they needed to do with that first £30 million. Since 1975, their engineers had been looking at replacing the old six-cylinder engine with the much more powerful 3.5-litre V8 that was already available in Range Rovers and Rover cars. The project was quickly brought to production readiness and the new model – inevitably known as the "Stage 1 V8" after the capital that paid for it – was announced at the Geneva Show in March 1979. At first it was available only for export, but UK sales followed in autumn 1980.

There was a certain irony about the sequence of events. The V8 was an all-alloy engine that had been bought from General Motors' Buick division in 1965, originally with the intention of fitting it to US-market Land Rovers, where extra power was desperately needed. Once it reached Solihull, the engine was hi-jacked by the cars side of the house and Land Rovers had to wait another 14 years to get it. In the meantime, it had also gone into the hugely successful Range Rover that was announced in 1970 – and, of course, into the 101 One Tonne military Forward Control.

However, putting the V8 engine into Land Rovers was not the only change as Land Rover Ltd got into its stride. The company also reworked its two four-cylinder engines, giving them five main bearings instead of three to promote both smoother running and longer life. The revised engines entered production in mid-1980 for the 1981 model-year. In Australia and South Africa, meanwhile, the local importers gained Solihull's agreement to buy-in engines that met local requirements better than those provided as standard. So the Australians bought in a 3.9-litre Isuzu diesel for the 109, and the South Africans bought in a 3.8-litre diesel and used a locally-made 2.6-litre petrol from the Leyland stable.

*The more powerful V8-engined Land Rover was expected to have special appeal in the Middle East, and all the pictures on the cover of the first sales brochure in 1979 were shot there. As late as 1982, pictures from that shoot were still being used. The one of the blue vehicle with divers shows the large "Land Rover V8" side decals used on the first models; the blue, plus a bright yellow and a bright green, were taken from the Triumph cars palette with the aim of livening up the appearance while the V8 engine livened up the performance.*

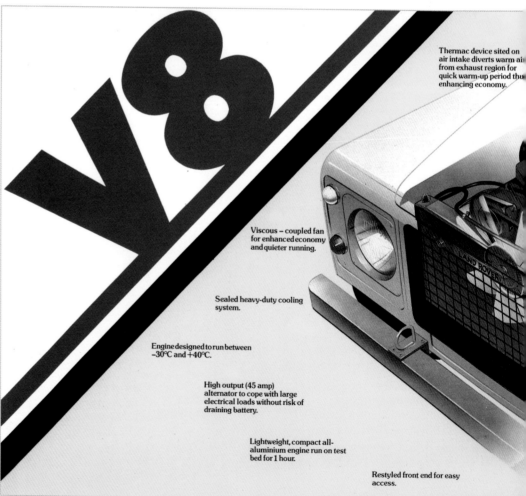

A yellow Land Rover was something of a shock to the system at the end of the 1970s. So was the new flush front with its black mesh grille, which helped give the V8-engined models a clear identity. The engine had indeed been seen in the Range Rover, but it was not the same; while the Range Rover had 125bhp, the Land Rover had just 91bhp, mainly because of worries about stopping with drum brakes on a laden vehicle from the V8's higher speeds.

*Different images suit different audiences, as this August 1980 catalogue for the UK market made clear. Though the news of the V8 was undeniably prominent, the example pictured was as dark, dull and worthily employed as Land Rovers had always been.*

*The V8 engine nestled comfortably within the engine bay, which had been widened to improve access for servicing.*

*Solihull's military division got the new V8 model ready for their customers as soon as they possibly could. The green fields and trees in the background suggest that, despite the sand tyres, this LHD model had not strayed from the UK for photography.*

Air cleaner incorporates one-way drain valve to prevent accumulation of water/dirt while wading.

Carburation and lubrication system arranged so engine is never starved of petrol/oil during violent manoeuvres.

Low compression ratio allows use of fuel down to 85 octane.

Self-adjusting tappets for quieter running.

Electical system PVC insulated thus giving protection against petrol, oil, moisture or fungal attack.

Crankshaft vibration damper ensures smoother running.

## V8 Power.

*The selling-point of the V8 engine was power, although actually it was the huge reserves of torque that were called upon to tow the military-pattern Bedford RL truck in the picture.*

The picture you see above is just one example of the massive power of the V8 Land-Rover.

The tried and tested V8 engine delivers 166lb/ft torque at 2000 rpm, yet its aluminium construction makes it 60% lighter than a cast iron equivalent.

This 90 bhp engine is housed in a completely redesigned engine compartment so that all service points are easily accessible. The ignition components are positioned at the highest level so that, even when the vehicle is wading through rivers, all important electrical components stay safely dry.

The air intake system has been designed to deliver optimum airflow to the carburettors while screening out the sand and dust that so often permeate a working environment.

With eight cylinders, the power is delivered very smoothly, quietly and with minimum vibration. Indeed for sheer reliability, this engine is unsurpassed.

The V8 Land-Rover is, quite literally, the most powerful Land-Rover you can buy. And everything else about the vehicle – the chassis, suspension and the controls – is built for truly heavy duty, allowing you to use that power to its limits. Making it ideal for such strenuous tasks as breakdown recovery as well as fire brigade, police, ambulance and military work.

# V8 Design and Construction.

If you were to visit the factory and watch a V8 Land-Rover being built, you would soon discover why the Land-Rover has become the world's most famous and most wanted four-wheel-drive vehicle.

In the design studio, 30 years of refining and improving the basic Land-Rover design has culminated in a range of rugged, rough country vehicles that is the envy of every other manufacturer.

Every part, every component, every body pressing is built to withstand more stress than it is ever likely to receive in a long, hard-working life.

The 'ladder' construction of the box section chassis gives an immensely strong foundation, capable of withstanding enormous shock for many years. What's more, this chassis is dip-painted so that it is protected both inside and out.

All the major body panels are of lightweight aluminium, which means they are completely resistant to corrosion. Most of these panels are bolted in position so that, in the event of denting, they can be very quickly replaced without your Land-Rover being taken out of commission. It is worth noting, too, that many of the parts are interchangeable with those of the Land-Rover and Range Rover.

Before it leaves the factory, every single Land-Rover is subjected to gruelling tests, on Land-Rover's own test track.

If there are any weaknesses, these tests will soon find them. But there seldom are.

Every Land-Rover that leaves our factory has to live up to a great tradition of stamina, durability and hard work.

We make sure the V8 lives up to that tradition in every way.

*The text here is designed to make clear that Land Rover had by no means thrown the baby out with the bath water. More than 30 years of building Land Rovers hadn't gone to waste – it was only the engine that was new. Well, almost. Catalogues didn't make much of it at the time, but the new V8 Land Rover also came with the Range Rover's permanent four-wheel-drive system instead of the selectable system of the earlier models. Once the Series IIIs had been replaced by the coil-sprung One Ten models, permanent four-wheel-drive was promoted as part of the essential Land Rover DNA.*

*The arrival of the V8 wasn't the final engine upgrade for the Series III models. From mid-1980, the two four-cylinder engines were updated with five main bearings instead of three. Interestingly, this 1982 catalogue refers to the new five-bearing types as 2¼-litre engines; Land Rover usually called them 2.3-litre types to make the distinction between old and new.*

# LAND ROVER
# engines & transmissions

2¼ litre Petrol

2¼ litre Diesel

All engines are designed to produce the flexibility required to satisfy the many different conditions under which Land Rovers operate.

The engines develop high torque at low engine speeds — just what is needed for all off-road duties and yet still have good road performance. It also helps to prolong the engine's working life.

All rotating and reciprocating parts are carefully balanced to give smooth running and long life. Each completed engine is fully tested before being installed.

The lubrication and carburation systems are sealed to protect the engine against adverse conditions such as sand, dust or water — this allows the vehicle to work on inclines of up to 45° or ford streams up to 1 metre deep.

Efficient filters protect the engine from damage when operating in dusty or sandy conditions.

All this is done to assure you of a reliable, trouble-free power unit with a long working life, and a good re-sale value.

2¼ litre petrol engines are also available in high and low-compression form to meet all octane levels.

An important function of Land Rover engines is the supply of power to run a wide range of auxiliary equipment. The engines are designed to overcome problems normally associated with stationary running and efficiently drive PTO equipment.

**5 Bearing Engines.** Recent developments of the 2¼ litre engines have resulted in both improved smooth running and reduced noise levels.

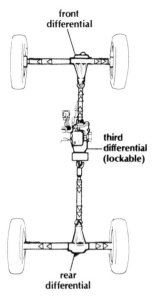

**Permanent 4 wheel drive for 3½ litre models**

front differential

third differential (lockable)

rear differential

*Land Rover plugged the V8 models for all it was worth in the early 1980s, and it's a V8 109 that takes pride of place on this more general sales leaflet for "closed cargo carriers" – hardtop models – from 1982.*

3½ litre Petrol

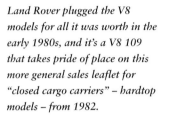

In South Africa, the new front-end panels designed for the Stage 1 V8 models were adopted as a distinguishing feature for two new models that arrived for the 1981 season. Though advertised here as "The new Series III", they were strictly Series IIIS types. Nobody ever called them that, though; to South African buyers they were known as R6 types after the R6 2.6-litre petrol engine that was fitted. This was a locally-built six-cylinder, related to an Austin-Morris engine. The diesel alternative was called the ADE4, and was a 3.8-litre four-cylinder of Perkins design built under licence by ADE (Atlantis Diesel Engines) in South Africa. Truck cab pick-ups were usually known by their Afrikaans name of "bakkie".

**Die nuwe Reeks III Land Rover**

**Die suksesverhaal word voortgesit**

# Die wêreld se veelsydigste voertuig

Die Land Rover is ongetwyfeld die veelsydigste voertuig ter wêreld. Aan geen ander ryding word die lewens van soveel mans en vroue toevertrou in digte, verafgeleë woude of in die onherbergsame woestynstreke van die wêreld nie. Geen ander werksesel is gewilliger vir so 'n groot verskeidenheid take as die Land Rover nie. Maak nie saak hoe woes, ruig of rof nie, die Land Rover kom altyd deur. Selfs op die grootpad lê hy rieme neer soos 'n wafferse sedanmotor. Maar dan word die Land Rover ook gebruik as kragbron vir plaasgereedskap en -implemente, is al in 'n skeertuig ombou en het ook as ambulans en brandweerwa diens gedoen. Hy's plaastrekker en gesinswa in een dag. Hy maak sy eie pad deur riviere, bosse en die steilste bulte. Hy ry waar geen ander voertuig dit durf waag nie.

Verkrygbaar in R6 petrol- of 4-silinder ADE-dieselenjin, stasiewa of bakkie, of in 'n

4-silinder petrolenjin (slegs bakkie). Alle modelle word gebou van roesbestande aluminiumbakke tesame met 'n duursame gegalvaniseerde onderstel vir enige denkbare gebruik. As 'n bus kan die Land Rover 12 passasiers met gemak vervoer. As bakkie tem hy die rofste paaie met tot twee ton op. Dis hierdie veelsydigheid wat Land Rover die gewilde keuse van private persone, munisipaliteite en selfs regerings oral in die wêreld maak. Betroubaarheid en kanniedood-werkverrigting, gekombineer met veelsydigheid — die legende leef voort in die Reeks III Land Rover.

**Doelgebou vir elke behoefte**
Daar's 'n Reeks III Land Rover wat presies aan u vereistes voldoen.

**Sessilinder petrol**
Die groot R6-enjin vir maksimum krag/verrigtingsbalans. Stuit vir niks nie. Verkrygbaar in 'n stasiewa sowel as bakkie.

**Viersilinder petrol**
Vir diegene wat 'n petrolenjin verkies met ware ekonomie, is hierdie model geskik vir ligter vragte en minder strawwe take. Slegs in 'n bakkie verkrygbaar.

**Viersilinder diesel**
Vir uithaler-ekonomie is die Atlantis-dieselenjin, ontwikkel in Suid-Afrika vir Suid-Afrikaanse toestande, onoortreflik. Verkrygbaar in 'n stasiewa sowel as bakkie.

# SPECIFICATIONS.

## Land Rover 109 Wheelbase, series III 3-9D

### NOMINAL CHASSIS DIMENSIONS

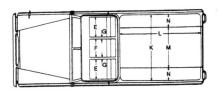

| | | mm | ins. |
|---|---|---|---|
| | Wheelbase | 2768 | 109.00 |
| | Track | 1334 | 52.50 |
| | Overall length | 4445 | 175.00 |
| | Overall width (over hinges) | 1680 | 66.00 |
| | Overall height of cab | 2006 | 75.50 |
| | Overall height with hood | 1980 | 78.00 |
| | Ground clearance | 209 | 8.25 |
| A | Front cushion to accelerator pedal | 468 | 17.25 |
| B | Front squab to steering wheel | 350 | 14.50 |
| C | Headroom front seat (uncomp.) | 991 | 39.00 |
| D | Front to rear of front cushion | 420 | 16.00 |

| | | mm | ins. |
|---|---|---|---|
| E | Width of front cushion | 460 | 18.00 |
| F | Width of front centre cushion | 380 | 15.00 |
| G | Width between front seats | 25 | 1.00 |
| H | Top of front cushion to floor | 380 | 14.50 |
| I | Front squab height | 540 | 17.00 |
| J | Height of body sides | 495 | 19.50 |
| K | Width of body interior | 444 | 56.87 |
| L | Length of body interior | 1850 | 72.75 |
| M | Interior body width between wheel boxes | 920 | 36.25 |
| N | Width of wheel boxes | 254 | 10.00 |
| O | Height of wheel boxes | 229 | 9.00 |

**HARDTOP**

**TRUCK**

**CHASSIS CAB**

**STATION WAGON**

**UTILITY**

**ENGINE**
Diesel
No. of Cylinders — 4
Bore — 102 mm
Stroke — 118 mm
Capacity — 3856 c.c.
Compression Ratio — 17:1
Max. Power — 72 kW @ 3200 R.P.M.
Max. torque — 255 Nm @ 1900 R.P.M.

**LUBRICATION SYSTEM**
Pressurised by submerged gear type pump. Red warning light on instrument panel when pressure drops below 69 kPa. Filtration through gauze intake pump filter in sump plus external full flow filter. Oil capacity 9.5 litres including 0.5 litre in filter.
OIL COOLER — Plate tube type located on right hand side of the cylinder block cooled by engine cooling water.

*The Stage 1 V8 chassis proved very popular with conversions specialists, adding performance where previously there had been nothing worthy of the name. This was one of the long-serving ambulance designs by Herbert Lomas, now installed on the V8-powered Land Rover. The example illustrated seems to have been intended for a military customer somewhere in the Middle East. The inscription "Approved by the Rover Company Limited" was rather out of date by the time this flyer was printed.*

*The Australian Isuzu-engined model was known as a 3.9D. In most other respects, it was standard Series III, but it had the permanent four-wheel-drive system of the Stage 1 V8. This August 1981 flyer, the first issued for the model, shows that the "truck" variant – not available from Solihull – was staple fare in Australia. Its body was normally made of aluminium, but wooden versions could also be ordered.*

# COUNTY AND HI-CAP

As the 1980s got under way, it was becoming obvious that four-wheel drive vehicles were rapidly becoming fashionable. A new group of buyers was taking an interest in them, largely as a knock-on effect of the Range Rover's success. The vehicles were becoming identified with outdoor activities and adventure sports, and as Japanese makers began to offer more car-like models, so buyers began to think of 4x4s as a genuine alternative to ordinary family estate cars.

Land Rover got in on the act from April 1982 with better-equipped versions of its Station Wagons, which were known as County types. Luxury models they were not, but by comparison with standard Station Wagons they did have an array of more "civilised" features. Cloth instead of vinyl upholstery was just the start. Adjustable front seats with head restraints, and a cubby box for oddments stowage, added to interior amenities. New paint colours and side decals – a fashion introduced by Japanese makers – also set these models apart from the crowd.

There was a second threat from Japanese 4x4 makers at the start of the 1980s, and Land Rover announced its response to that in April 1982 as well. The threat was from rugged pick-up trucks, which offered most of the advantages of the 109-inch truck cab Land Rover at lower prices – and added better performance and more comfort at the same time. For the moment, the best Land Rover could do was to add a new body type to the 109 range, which offered more load space. When ordered with the heavy-duty suspension option as well, it gave a payload of up to 1.3 tons.

The new body style was called the High Capacity Pick-Up, and Land Rover tended to shorten the name to HCPU although users mostly called it the Hi-Cap. It was recognisable from outside by flatter sides and a wider tailgate than the standard pick-up body (which remained available), and more space was achieved inside by replacing the wheelboxes with simple wheel arches.

*Side stripes and new colours identified the County Station Wagons from the outside. On the 88s, there were auxiliary driving lamps with plastic lens covers as well. The new interiors were an important element in moving the County specification away from the workhorse ambience of the standard Land Rover.*

# Land Rover *County*

The Land Rover County Station Wagon available in short and long wheelbase form is the latest addition to the Land Rover range. With its impressive appearance it incorporates many new features which make it an extremely high specification on or off road vehicle.

The County Station Wagon is ideally suited to the private user wanting a versatile and reliable four wheel drive vehicle for leisure, work or the transportation of his family. Equally the County is attractive to the commercial user where a higher specification vehicle is required.

## TYRES

The current range of approved tyres are available on the 2710 kg GVW version. For the 3020 kg GVW High-Load the standard tyre is the Avon Range Ranger. MK₂-6 ply.

Optional tyres available are:
- Michelin XS.
- Michelin XC4 8 ply radial.
- Michelin XCL.
- Dunlop RTM 8 ply (not V8).
- Avon Range Master Radial

## OPTIONAL EQUIPMENT

A wide range of accessories are available to meet all your requirements.

Specific items are:
- ¾ length canvas hood.
- 7 pin trailer socket and plug.
- Mudflaps.
- Towing drop plate/jaw/hook/ball.
- County seats.
- County acoustic trim.
- Cubby box (only in certain markets).

See your local Dealer for a complete list of the options and accessories available.

| ENGINE | BORE | STROKE | CAP-ACITY | MAX TORQUE | MAX POWER | TRANSMISSION |
|---|---|---|---|---|---|---|
| 2¼ litre Petrol | 90.47 mm | 88.9 mm | 2286 cm³ | (117lbf.ft) at 2000 rpm | 51.5kw/ 69bhp at 4000 rpm | Selectable 4 wheel drive |
| 3½ litre Petrol | 88.9 mm | 71.1 mm | 3528 cm³ | (166.5lbf.ft) at 2000 rpm | 67.7kw/ 90.7bhp at 3500 rpm | Permanent four wheel drive through centre 3rd diff. |
| 2¼ litre Diesel | 90.47 mm | 88.9 mm | 2286 cm³ | (103lbf.ft) at 1800 rpm | 448kw/60bhp at 4000 rpm | Selectable 4 wheel drive |

Bed length  A = 2.01m (79")
Bed width   B = 1.63m (64")
Bed width   C = 0.92m (36")

It was only to be expected that the sales leaflet would show a V8-engined Hi-Cap on the front, as Land Rover saw its V8 models as the flagships of the range. The back page showed the real world, where most buyers bought four-cylinder types. They would probably have bought V8s if they could, but the initial purchase price was higher and the running costs were inflated by quite alarmingly high fuel consumption. By 1982, 15mpg was next to anti-social.

## PAYLOAD DATA

| Model | EEC Kerb Weight | | | | EEC Payload | | | | Non EEC Kerb Weight | | | | Non EEC Payload | | | |
|---|---|---|---|---|---|---|---|---|---|---|---|---|---|---|---|---|
| | 2710kg | | 3020kg | | 2710kg | | 3020kg | | 2710kg | | 3020kg | | 2710kg | | 3020kg | |
| | kgs | lbs | kgs | lbs | kgs | lbs | kgs | lbs | kgs | lbs | kgs | lbs | kgs | lbs | kgs | lbs |
| 2¼ Petrol | 1627 | 3586 | 1686 | 3709 | 1083 | 2387 | 1334 | 2941 | 1503 | 3313 | 1562 | 3436 | 1207 | 2660 | 1458 | 3214 |
| 2¼ Diesel | 1676 | 3694 | 1719 | 3782 | 1034 | 2279 | 1301 | 2868 | 1544 | 3403 | 1587 | 3498 | 1166 | 2570 | 1433 | 3158 |
| 3½ Petrol | 1674 | 3689 | 1717 | 3777 | 1036 | 2283 | 1303 | 2873 | 1550 | 3416 | 1593 | 3505 | 1160 | 2557 | 1427 | 3146 |

**Note:** EEC Kerb Weights—are the minimum vehicle specification + full tank and 75 kg driver.
Non-EEC Kerb Weights—are the minimum vehicle specification excluding driver and fuel.

| TOWING WEIGHTS | P 4 cyl | | D 4 cyl | | P 8 cyl | |
|---|---|---|---|---|---|---|
| | On road | Off road | On road | Off road | On road | Off road |
| Trailer without brakes | 500kg | 500kg | 500kg | 500kg | 500kg | 500kg |
| Trailer with overrun brakes | 2000kg 4410lb | 1000kg 2205lb | 2000kg 4410lb | 1000kg 2205lb | 2000kg 4410lb | 1000kg 2205lb |
| 4 wheel trailer with continuous or semi-continuous brakes. i.e. coupled brakes | 4000kg 8820lb | 1000kg 2205lb | 3000kg 6615lb | 1000kg 2205lb | 4000kg 8820lb | 1000kg 2205lb |

Advised trailer nose weight limit 75 kg.

 **Land Rover Ltd**
Lode Lane, Solihull, West Midlands, England. Telephone: 021-743 4242 Telex: Lan Rov G338641 Cables Rover Solihull

PRINTED IN ENGLAND LR/199/2.82/70M(B)

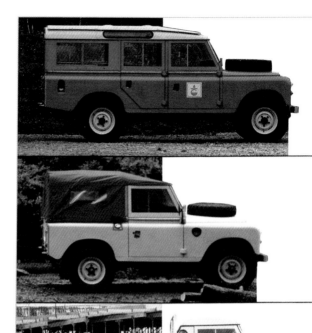

### Fleet Versatility

For every requirement in your fleet, there's a Land Rover to do the job. Land Rover offers from 2 to 12 seat alternatives, and secure Hard Top and Pick-Up versions for the transport of goods and materials with excellent towing capabilities. They are built to go anywhere, and designed for profitable operation. They need the minimum of maintenance; the famous rust-free Land Rover bodywork, with reliable, long-life engines, means a high re-sale value. Commonality of components reduces spares stocking and replacement costs, resulting in major cost savings for you and minimal downtime.

The Land Rover has also been closely associated with the increasing growth of leisure activities. Where towing or personnel carrying is important no other vehicle can match its suitability and versatility.

### Forestry

Land Rover's tenacious four-wheel drive surmounts practically all obstacles, carrying or towing heavy loads where only beasts of burden were previously considered suitable. And Land Rover is designed to be just as economical, with the toughness and reliability essential for continual, heavy multi-purpose work — whatever the conditions.

### Building & Civil Engineering

The transport of men, materials and equipment, often across the roughest of terrains is essential for the efficiency of many building projects. Land Rover, with its four-wheel drive power, can do it, with a bonus — the versatility of powering a range of equipment through its multi-purpose power take-off facilities. This is the adaptability and reliability, with low maintenance requirements, that has made Land Rover the workhorse of the world.

### Emergency Services

Motorway patrol vehicle, ambulance, fire tender: Land Rover has been chosen for all of these roles. Because Land Rover has the load-carrying capacity, combined with the ability to get to the scene of an emergency whatever the obstacles — essential qualities in isolated areas, and in all off-road situations. It is sure-footed enough to climb a motorway bank, powerful enough for the recovery of vehicles many times its size, and with its PTO systems, versatile enough to power items such as winches, pumps, lighting, welding and cutting equipment.

### Military

There is a long and varied history of Land Rover in Army, Air Force, Navy and security applications throughout the world. Land Rover is a vehicle that can take the roughest treatment, and still be depended upon in a tough situation. And it has the versatility of no other vehicle. Land Rovers have been used in almost every conceivable role — personnel carrier, armoured car, communications, mobile forward command post — even as a half-track. It's probably the single most useful vehicle at the disposal of any force.

### Agriculture

Land Rover four-wheel drive can get you to any part of your farm, plantation or estate whatever the conditions. And the Land Rover PTO facility means that you can do a multitude of jobs without assistance. Land Rover is more than just a vehicle; it's an extremely versatile, mobile power unit. Low maintenance costs, non-rusting alloy body, rugged construction and long-life engine — all these combine to give you reliable, economic service day after day, year after year.

*Away from the urbanised County models, Land Rover was still selling strongly to its traditional customers, even though sales had collapsed in Africa during the early 1980s under the onslaught from cheap Japanese 4x4s. These images showed how Land Rover saw their marketplace in 1982.*

# COILS TAKE OVER

The transition from leaf springs to coil springs was gradual. Coil springs had demonstrated their value on the Range Rover in the 1970s, and Solihull had worked towards adding them to Land Rovers as well from the middle of that decade. First came the One Ten – "Land Rover's new Land Rover" – with a 110-inch wheelbase. Announced in March 1983, it replaced the Stage 1 V8 109s immediately, but the four-cylinder Series IIIs remained in low-volume production for export until the last one was built in mid-1985.

Then in 1984, it was the turn of the short-wheelbase models to be replaced. The new coil-sprung model was called a Ninety (although its wheelbase was actually 92.9 inches). Like the One Ten, it was recognisably derived from the Series III, the main recognition feature being wheelarch "eyebrows" to cover wider tracks.

The Ninety and One Ten, renamed Defender 90 and Defender 110 in 1990, remained in production as this book went to press in 2013.

*The tag-line on the first sales catalogue for the new One Ten said it all. This was "Land Rover's new Land Rover" – nothing more and nothing less.*

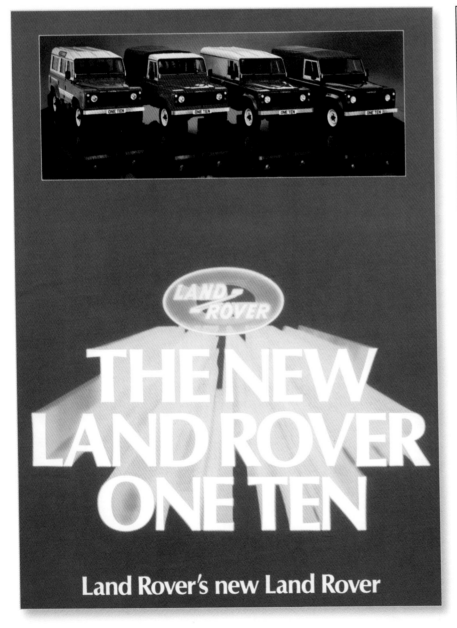

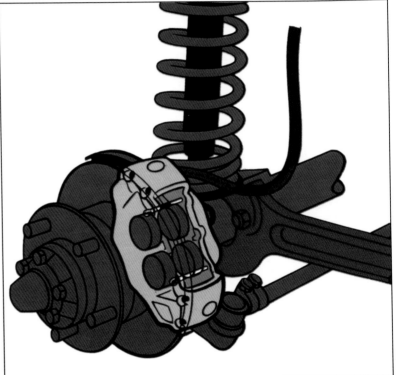

*The One Ten brought not only coil springs but also disc brakes at the front for the first time. Although a few were built with the selectable four-wheel-drive system of the Series III, it was not long before all had the permanent four-wheel-drive system that had always been intended as one of their key features.*

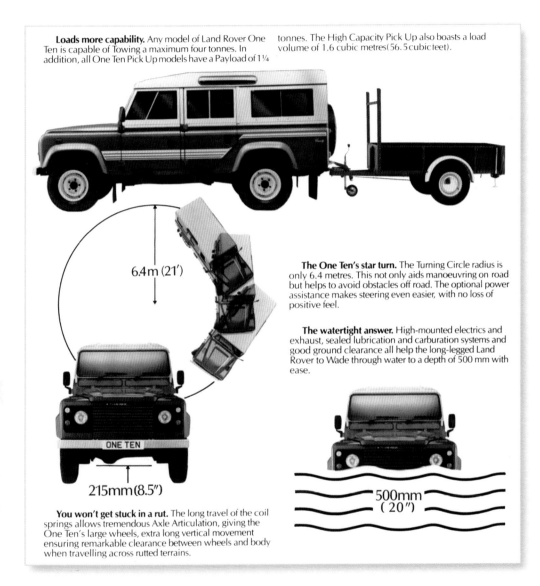

**Loads more capability.** Any model of Land Rover One Ten is capable of Towing a maximum four tonnes. In addition, all One Ten Pick Up models have a Payload of 1¼ tonnes. The High Capacity Pick Up also boasts a load volume of 1.6 cubic metres (56.5 cubic feet).

6.4m (21')

**The One Ten's star turn.** The Turning Circle radius is only 6.4 metres. This not only aids manoeuvring on road but helps to avoid obstacles off road. The optional power assistance makes steering even easier, with no loss of positive feel.

**The watertight answer.** High-mounted electrics and exhaust, sealed lubrication and carburation systems and good ground clearance all help the long-legged Land Rover to Wade through water to a depth of 500 mm with ease.

215mm (8.5")

500mm (20")

**You won't get stuck in a rut.** The long travel of the coil springs allows tremendous Axle Articulation, giving the One Ten's large wheels, extra long vertical movement ensuring remarkable clearance between wheels and body when travelling across rutted terrains.

*Though photographs were the order of the day by 1983, the presentation in sales brochures was bright and modern. The vehicle is a One Ten County Station Wagon; the characteristic wheelarch "eyebrows" are obvious in these pictures.*

*Leaf-sprung models remained available alongside the coil-sprung One Ten for a time. Though the top two pictures show One Ten models, the two below are a Series III 88 and Series III 109.*